COLLOQUIAL HIND

Kaka Kalelkar's commendation of this little volume is entirely well deserved. Indeed the book is in no need of any recommendation at all. Suiting all pockets, in size and price here is a collection of 1224 short conversational sentences grouped under 33 heads. Each sentence in Hindi carries its equivalent in Gujarati, Marathi, and English. The contents are thus altogether wider and more useful than the title indicates. They cover conversational Gujarati and conversational Marathi as well as conversational Hindi.

The adoption of a standard Devanagari script is a big help in removing such genuine difficulty or prejudice against Hindi as exists in many parts of the country; and one profoundly hopes that Gujarat's wise and courageous decision to adopt the Devanagari script for Gujarati is only a pioneer step in the speedy and universal adoption of that script for all Indian languages.

In the situation in which we find ourselves today, there is need for each one of us to become a minor linguist with working knowledge of at least three Indian languages including Hindi. Shri Jain's book is a helpful step in that direction. The close affinity here disclosed between Hindi and Gujarati, for instance, comes as a happy surprise to the Marathi reader.

In his preface, the author has made the welcome announcement that versions of this book will be produced in different Indian languages. The choice of the conversational sentence is made on the basis of Hindi idiom, and therefore will not need to be changed for the different linguistic versions. The selection itself is remarkably comprehensive and must have obviously involved long and diligent labour.

—BHARAT JYOTI

Conversational
Hindi

Includes Gujarati & Marathi

Narayan Prasad Jain

JAICO PUBLISHING HOUSE

Mumbai • Delhi • Bangalore • Kolkata
Hyderabad • Chennai • Ahmedabad • Bhopal

Published by Jaico Publishing House
121 Mahatma Gandhi Road
Mumbai - 400 001
jaicopub@vsnl.com
www.jaicobooks.com

© Jaico Publishing House

CONVERSATIONAL HINDI
ISBN 81-7224-275-1

Eleventh Jaico Impression: 2007

Printed by
Efficient Offset Printers
215, Shahzada Bagh Industrial Complex
Phase -ll, Delhi-110035

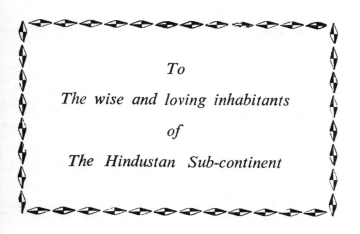

To

The wise and loving inhabitants

of

The Hindustan Sub-continent

PREFACE

As a teacher of Hindi I have seen that most students, even after passing their 'degree' examinations, remain woefully deficient in conversational Hindi. This book aims at minimising that deficiency.

It is a preliminary presentation, in colloquial form of the Hindi as envisaged in the Constitution of India. It is free from far-fetched Sanskrit, Arabic or Persian words. It is basic Hindi.

Bolti Hindi also serves as a self-instructor for conversational Gujarati, Marathi and English.

It has been prepared primarily with a view to meeting the linguistic requirements of cosmopolitan Bombay. I think it will be read with interest by English-speaking people too who seem to appreciate only simple, lucid Hindi. It will also be of help to those students who have to offer a provincial language as a subjtect for their higher Hindi examinations.

An antidote to linguistic fanaticism, which tends to disintegrate India, is universal propagation of liberal Hindi as exemplified in this book. To enrich Hindi the protagonists of Hindi too should learn other Indian languages, all of which should be written and printed in Devanagari script. This reform brooks no delay. Consequently, Gujarati is here printed in Devanagari script. In other editions also, covering the remaining languages of India, I propose to use the Devanagari Script.

My acknowledgments are due to the authors of the books I have consulted, and the friends who have helped me to bring out this book. In particular my heartfelt thanks are due to my great friend Rev. H. O. Mascarenhas, M.A., PH.D., D.D., for his very valuable assistance in preparing the last lesson of this book.

My heartfelt thanks are also due to Kumari Leila Bawdekar, M.A., for her invaluable help in revising the entire book and in correcting the Marathi lines in the light of the latest improvements, in Marathi grammar, carried out by the Maharashtra Government and the Marathi Sahitya Parishad.

I am grateful to Karmavir Pandit Sunder Lalji for the Foreword, and to Padmavibhushan Kaka Saheb Kaleklar for the Introduction, which is an ample reward and encouragement to me.

Even if two persons separated by linguistic barriers come closer by reading this little book, I shall deem myself abundantly compensated.

Study of our regional languages besides being a great delight and thorough enjoyment, is highly conducive to national integration and emotional unity. Let us, therefore, willingly and gladly learn the languages of our country.

Narayan Prasad Jain

Banarsi Mansion
Malad, Bombay

यह हिन्दी है

श्री नारायण प्रसाद जैन ने मुझे अपनी पुस्तक 'बोलती हिन्दी' दिखलाई. मैंने उसे ध्यान से पढ़ा. इसमें कोई सन्देह नहीं कि इस किताब का लेखक खड़ी बोली, हिन्दी, के मुहावरे से पूरी तरह वाक़िफ है. पुस्तक भर में एक भी वाक्य ऐसा नहीं है जिसे बोलचाल की निगाह से ग़लत कहा जा सके. किताब सचमुच बोलती हिन्दी है ! इसकी हिन्दी ठीक वह हिन्दी है जो हमारे देश का विधान चाहता है, जिसे सब हिन्दी-भाषी गली-कूचों और गाँवों में बोलते हैं, जिसे राष्ट्रपिता महात्मा गांधी राष्ट्रभाषा बनाना चाहते थे. जो सचमुच हमारी राष्ट्रभाषा होने के काबिल है. हर वाक्य इतना आसान है कि किसी को मत-लब बताने की ज़रूरत नहीं हो सकती. लेखक ने हिन्दी वाक्यों के साथ-साथ गुजराती, मराठी और अंग्रेजी वाक्य देकर पुस्तक के मूल्य और उसकी उपयोगिता को और भी बढ़ा दिया है. जिन देशवासियों के दिलों में राष्ट्रभाषा हिन्दी से प्रेम है और जो सचमुच जीती-जागती बोलचाल की हिन्दी जानना और सीखना चाहते हैं उनके लिये इससे अच्छी पुस्तक नहीं हो सकती.

मैं चाहता हूँ कि श्री नारायण प्रसाद जैन इसी तरह की और भी पुस्तकें लिखें, ताकि 'बोलती हिन्दी' की

एक माला तैयार हो जाए जो हमारे सब स्कूलों में टेक्स्ट बुक का काम दे सके—अहिन्दी-भाषी प्रान्तों में हिन्दी के ज़रिये दूसरी भारतीय भाषाएँ सीखने के लिये.

मैं देश की सब सरकारों और शिक्षा-संस्थाओं से पूरे ज़ोर के साथ सिफ़ारिश करता हूँ और अनुरोध करता हूँ कि वह इस सुन्दर पुस्तक को अपनावें और उसके प्रचार और फैलाव में हर तरह मदद करें ।

—सुन्दरलाल

आमुख

'बोलती हिन्दी' एक अच्छा, उपयोगी प्रकाशन है। पश्चिम भारत को खास ध्यान में रखकर बनाया गया है। किन्तु भारत के दूसरे प्रदेश के लोग भी इससे अच्छा लाभ उठा सकते हैं।

रोज़मर्रा के व्यवहार में काम में आनेवाले हर तरह के हज़ार या डेढ़ हज़ार वाक्य लेकर उनका हिन्दी, गुजराती, मराठी और अंग्रेज़ी अनुवाद इसमें दिया है।

मुझे विश्वास है कि इस प्रकाशन की खूबी और उसका लाभ ध्यान में आते ही भारत की दूसरी भाषा बोलनेवाले लोग भी इसका अनुकरण करेंगे।

यह छोटा सा ग्रंथ बाक़ायदा पढ़ने के लायक़ तो है ही। लेकिन जिनके पास फ़ुरसत नहीं है ऐसे लोग भी इसे खरीदकर अपने पास रख सकते हैं और जब कभी समय मिले इधर-उधर पढ़ सकते हैं और याद करके दूसरे भी ऐसे वाक्य तैयार कर सकते हैं।

१५०० वाक्यों में इतनी विविधता है कि मनुष्य को जो भी कहना हो, समझाना हो, इन्हीं की मदद से नये-नये वाक्य बनाकर वह अपने भाव प्रकट कर सकता है।

श्री नारायण प्रसाद जैन की हिन्दी की सेवा, हिन्दुस्तानी की सेवा, नई बात नहीं है। बहुत बरसों के

अनुभव और चिंतन से उन्होंने यह किताब बनाई है। उसका पुरस्कार करते मुझे बड़ी खुशी होती है। 'जैको' प्रकाशन संस्था को भी धन्यवाद दिये बिना मैं नहीं रह सकता। मुझ विश्वास है कि स्वराज्य नगरी बम्बई, नज़दीक के भविष्य में हिन्दी का एक सर्वसामान्य प्रधान केन्द्र बनेगी।

—काका कालेलकर

विषय-सूची (Contents)

बोलती हिन्दी

CONVERSATIONAL HINDI

1. प्रारंभिक (Elementary)

समझे ?
Samjhay ?
समज्या ?
समजलात ?
Do you understand ?

जी हाँ. (हाँ जी.)
Jee haan (*Haan jee*)
हा जी.
होय.
Yes. I do.

जी नहीं. (नहीं जी.)
Jee Naheen. (*Naheen jee*)
ना जी.
नाही.
No, I don't.

डरो मत.
Daro mat.
डरो नहीं.
घाबरू नका.
Don't be afraid.

सामने देखो.
Saamne daikho.
सामे जुओ.
समोर बघा.
Look ahead.

आगे बढ़ो.
Aagay badho.
आगल वधो.
पुढें चला.
Go ahead.

कोशिश करो.
Koshish karo.
प्रयत्न करो.
प्रयत्न करा.
Try.

सुरेश है क्या !
Suresh hai kya ?
सुरेश छे के ?
सुरेश आहे काय ?
Is Suresh in ?

साहब हैं ?
Sahab hain ?
साहेब छे ?
साहेब आहेत ?
Is the boss (master) in ?

कौन है ?
Kaun hai ?
कोण छे ?
कोण आहे ?
Who is it ?

मैं रमेश हूँ.
Men Ramesh hoon.
हुं रमेश छुं.
मी रमेश आहे.
It's Ramesh.

क्या है ?
Kya hai ?
शुं छे ?
काय आहे ?
What is it ?

दिनेश कहाँ गया ?
Dinesh kahan gaya ?
दिनेश क्यां गयो ?
दिनेश कोठे गेला आहे ?
Where is Dinesh ?

मालूम नहीं कहाँ चले गये.
Maaloom nahin kahan chale gaye.
खबर नथी क्यां चाल्यो गयो.
ठाऊक नाही कोठे गेले आहेत.
I don't know where he is.

जा मालूम नहीं.
Jee, maaloom nahin.
जा खबर नथी.
माहीत नाही
I don't know.

जरा ठहरिये.
Zaraa thahariye.
जरा ऊभा रहो.
जरा थांबा.
Please wait.

नज़दीक (क़रीब, पास) आइये.
Nazdeek (kareeb, pass) aiye.
पासे आवो.
जवळ या.
Please come closer.

साल मुबारक.
Saal mubarak.
साल मुबारक.
नूतन वर्षाभिनंदन.
Happy New Year.

कैसे हो ?
Kesay ho ?
केम छो ?
कसे काय ?
How are you ?

अच्छा हूँ.
Achchha hoon.
ठीक छे.
ठीक आहे.
I am well.

कब आये ?
Kab aaye ?
क्यारे आव्या ?
केव्हा आलात ?
When did you arrive ?

चलो, खेलें.
Chalo khaillen.
चालो रमीए.
चला खेलू या.
Come, let's play !

शुरू करें ?
Shuroo karen ?
शुरू करीए ?
सुरू करु या ?
Shall we begin ?

कौन जीता ?
Kaun jeeta ?
कोण जीत्यु
कोण जिंकल
Who won ?

क्या हुआ ?
Kya hua ?
शुं थयुं ?
काय झाले ?
What happend ?

कुछ नहीं.
Kuchh naheen.
कांई नहीं.
काही नहीं.
Nothing.

मैं जाऊँ ?
Men jaaoon ?
हुं जाऊँ ?
मी जाऊ ?
May I go ?

मैं भी चलूँ ?
Men bhi chaloon ?
हुं पण आवुं
मी सुद्धा येऊ ?
May I join you ? (go with you)

तुम आत्ते हो ?
Tum aatay ho ?
तमे आवो छो ?
तुम्ही येता ?
Are you coming ?

देर मत करो.
Dair mat karo.
वार लगाडो नहीं. मोडुं करो मा.
उशीर करू नका.
Don't delay !

जो अज्ञा. बहुत अच्छा.
Jo aagya. Bahut achchha.
जेवो हुकम.
जशी आज्ञा.
As you say (sir or madam).

मैं लाऊँ ?
Men laaoon ?
हुं लावुं ?
मी आणू ?
Shall I bring it ?

तुम नहीं मानोगे ?
Tum nahen maanogay ?
तुं नहि माने ?
तुम्ही ऐकणार नाही ?
Won't you listen ?

क्या बकते हो !
Kya baktay ho.
शुं बको छो !
काय बडबडाता आहात !
What a nonsense !

वापस जाओ.
Vaapas jaao.
पाछा जाव.
परत फिरा.
Go back.

वापस जाओ.
Vaapas jao.
पाछा आओ.
परत या.
Please come back.

हाथ धोओ.
Hath dhoo.
हाथ धुओ.
हात धुवा.
Wash your hands.

जल्दी आना.
Jaldee aana.
जल्दी आवो.
लवकर या.
Come soon.

गाड़ी रोको.
Gaadee roko.
गाड़ी उभी रखो.
गाड़ी थांबबा.
Stop the car (carriage, train)

ज़ोर लगाइये.
Zoar lagaiye.
जोर लगावो.
जोर करा.
Use your strength. Try harder.

जाने दीजिये.
Jaanay deejive.
जवा दो.
जाऊ द्या.
Let it pass.

और कुछ ?
Aur kuchh ?
बीजु काई ?
आणखी नाही ?
Anything else ? What else ?

अहा !
Aha !
अहाहा !
अहाहा !
Aha ?

वाह वाह !
Vaah vaah !
वाह वाह !
वाहवा !
Marvellous ?

शाबाश !
Shaabaash !
शाबाश !
शाबास !
Well done ? Bravo ?

ख़बरदार !
Khabardaar !
ख़बरदार !
ख़बरदार !
Beware ?

अरे !
Aray !
अरे !
अरे !
Oh ?

हाय !
Hai !
हाय !
हाय !
Woe !

हे राम !
Hay Ram !
हे राम !
हे राम !
O God !

2. घरेलू (1) [Domestic (1)]

जरा देखो दरवाज़ा कौन खटखटा रहा है.
Zara daikho darwaza kaun khatkhata raha hai.
जरा जुओ, कोंण दरवाजो खटखटावे छे.
जरा पहा, दरवाजा कोण ठोठावते आहे.
Please see who is knocking at the door.

कोई मिलने आया है.
Kai milne aaya hai.
कोक मलवा आव्युं छे.
कोणोतरी भेटायला आला आहे.
Some one has come to see you.

उनका नाम पूछो.
Unka naam poochho.
तेमनुं नाम पूछा.
त्याचे नाव विचारा.
Ask him his name.

तशरीफ़ लाइये. आइये पधारिये.
Tashreef laaiye. Aaiye padhariye.
आओ, पधारो.
यावे, यावे. (या या)
Please come in.

तशरीफ़ रखिये. विराजिये.
Tashreaf rakhiye, Viraajie.
पधारो.
वसावे.
Please be seated.

कुर्सी ले लीजिए.
Kursi lay leejye.
खुरसी लो. खुरसी पर बेसो.
खुर्चीवर वसावे.
Take a chair, please.

आपका शुभ नाम ?
Aapka Shubh naam ?
आपनु नाम ?
आपले नाव, आपण कोण ?
Your name, please ?

मेरा नाम श्रीराम है.
Maira naam Shreeam hai
मारु नाम श्रीराम छे.
मला श्रीराम म्हणतात. माझे नाव श्रीराम.
My name is Shriram.

आपकी तारीफ़ ?
Aap ki taareef ?
आपनो परिचय ?
आपण कोण ?
who are you, please ?

ये लखनऊ के बाशिन्दे (निवासी) हैं.
Yay Lukhnaoo ke baashinde (niwaasi) hain.
ए लखनऊना रहेवासी छे.
हे लखनौचे रहिवासी आहेत.
He is a resident of Lucknow.

मिज़ाज शरीफ़ ?
Mizaaj Shareef ?
केम छो ?
कसे काय ?
How are you ? How do you do ?

बालबच्चे अच्छे हैं न ?
Baal—bachchay achchhe hain na ?
बालबच्चा मजामां छे ने ?
मुलेबाले ठीक आहेत ना ?
How is the family ? How are the children ?

आप तकलीफ़ न कीजिअे.
Aap takleef na keejiye.
तमे तकलीफ़ न करो.
आपण तसदी घेऊ नका.
Don't trouble yourself.

क्यों तकलीफ़ करते हैं ?
Kyon takleef karte hain ?
शा माटे कष्ट करो छो ?
कशाला तसदी घेता ?
Why take trouble ?

क्या खबर है ?
Kya khabar hai ?
शु ख़बर छे ?
काय खबर आहे ?
What's the news ?

कोई खास बात नहीं.
Ko khaas baat nahin.
कई खास नथी.
काही विशेष नाहीं.
Nothing in particular.

सब ठीक है.
Sab theek hai.
बधुं बराबर छे.
सर्व ठीक आहे.
All is well. Everything is alright.

क्या फ़रमाया ?
Kya farmaaya ?
शो हुकम छे ? शुं कह्यु
काय म्हणालात ? काय सांगितलेत
What did you say, sir or madam ?

हमारे यहाँ मेहमान आए हुए हैं.
Hamaaray yahaan mehmaan aaye huye hain.
अमारे त्यां म्हेमान आव्या छे.
आमच्याकडे पाहुणे आहेत.
We have some guests.

इजाजत दीजिये.
Ijaazet deejiye.
रजा आपो.
परवानगी द्या.
Allow me to go.

जरा और बैठिये.
Zaraa aur bethiye.
बेसो ने जरा.
आणखी थोडस बसाव. बसा हो थोडा वेळ.
Please stay a little longer.

मुझे फ़ुरसत नहीं.
Mujhe fursat Nahin.
मने वखत नथी.
मला सवड नाही.
I have no time.

माफ़ फ़र्माइये. माफ़ कीजिये. क्षमा कीजिये.
Maaf farmaaiye. Maaf keejiye. Kshmaa keejiye
माफ करो. क्षमा करो.
माफ करा. क्षमा करा. क्षमा करावी.
Please, excuse me. I am sorry.

आपकी कृपा (मेहरबानी) है.
Aapki krapaa (mehrbaani) hai.
तमारो कृपा (मेहरबानी) छे.
आपली कृपा (मेहरबानी) आहे.
By your grace. So kind of you.

आपकी बड़ी कृपा (मेहरबानी) होगी.

Aapki badi krapaa hogi.

तमारी मोटी मेहरबानी थशे.

आपली मोठी मेहरबानी होईल.

It would be very kind of you.

मैं आपकी क्या सेवा करूँ ?

Men aapki kya sewa karoon ?

हुं तमारी शी सेवा करूं ?

मी आपली काय सेवा करू ?

What shall I do for you ?

मुझे कुछ नहीं चाहिये.

Mujhe kuchh naheen chaahiye.

मारे कंई पण नथी जोईतुं.

मला काही नको.

I do not want anything.

बड़े दिनों के बाद दर्शन दिये.

Baday dinon kay baad darshan.

घणा दिवसे दर्शन थयां.

पुष्कळ दिवसांनंतर आपली भेट झाली.

We are meeting after a long time.

आप कैसे तशरीफ़ लाये ?

Aap kesy tashreef laaye ?

आपनुं पधारवुं केम थयुं ?

आपले येणे कसे झाले ? आपण कसे आलात ?

What brings you here ?

कैसे तकलीफ़ की (कष्ट किया) ?
Kesay takleef kec (kashta kiya) ?
केम आवबुं थयुं ?
का येणे झाले ?
What brings you here ?

आप से मशवरा लेना है.
Aapse mashwarac lena hai.
तमारी सलाह लेवी छे.
आपला सल्ला ध्यावयाचा आहे.
I want your abvice. I seek your advice.

आपकी क्या राय है ?
Aapki kya rai hui ?
तभारो शुं अभिप्राय छे ?
आपले काय मत आहे ?
What is your opinion ?

यह मैं कैसे कर सकता हूँ ?
Yeh men kesay kar saktaa hun ?
आ हुं केवी रीते करी शकीश ?
हे मी कसे करूं शकेन ?
How can I do this ?

मुझसे यह काम नहीं होगा.
Mujhse yeh kaam nahin hoga.
माराथी आ काम नहीं थाय.
माझ्याने हे काम होणार नाही.
I cannot do this.

यह नहीं हो सकता.
Yeh nahin ho sakta.
आ नहीं थई शके.
असे होऊ शकत नाही.
It cannot be.

ऐसा कैसे हो सकता है ?
Esaa kesay ho sakta hai ?
एम केम थई शके ?
असे कसे होऊ शकेल ?
How can it be so ?

बेहूदा न बको.
Baihooda na bako.
फावे तेम बको नहीं.
वाटेल ते बडबडू नका.
Don't talk nonsense.

आप क्या काम करते हैं ?
Aap kya kaam karte hain ?
तमे शुं काम करो छो ?
आपण काय काम करता ?
What are you ?

मुझे काम करने दो.
Mujhe kaam karne do.
मने काम करवा दो.
मला काम करू द्या.
Let me work.

यह काम खत्म करके चलता हूँ.

Yeh kaam khatma karke chaltaa hun.

आ काम पूरुं करीने आवुं छुं.

हे काम संपवून येतो.

Coming after finishing this work.

यह काम पूरा करके जाना.

Yeh kaam poora karke jaana.

आ काम पूरुं करीने जजो.

हे काम पूर्ण करून जा.

You may go after finishing this work.

इन लोगों को अपना काम करने दो.

In logon ko apna kaam karnc do.

आ लोकोने पोतानुं काम करवा दो.

या लोकांना त्यांचे काम करु द्या.

Let these people do their work.

अब मैं जाता हूँ, मुझे ज़रूरी काम है.

Ab men jaata hun, mujhe zaroori kaam hai.

हवे हुं जाऊं छुं, मारे जरूरी काम छे.

आता मी जातो, मला जरूरीचे काम आहे.

Now I must go, for I have some urgent work.

आप से एक खास काम है.

Aapse aik khaas kaam hai.

तमारुं एक खास काम छे.

आपल्याकडे एक विशेष काम आहे.

I have some important work with you.

इस वक़्त बहुत काम में हूँ.
Is waqt pahut kaam men hun.
અત્યારે ઘણા કામમાં છું.
मी कामात अगदी गढून गेला आहे.
(मी ह्या वेळी खूपच कामात गढलेला आहे.)
I am very busy now.

मैं ज़रूरी काम से आया हूँ.
Men zaroori kaam se aaya hun.
હું ખાસ કામ માટે આવ્યો છું.
मी आवश्यक (महत्त्वाच्या) कामासाठी आलो आहे.
I have come for some important work.

आपसे एक काम था.
Aapse aik kaam tha.
તમારું એક કામ હતું.
आपल्यापाशी एक काम होते.
I had some work with you.

वे आएँ तो बिठाना.
Way aayen tau bithaana.
તેઓ આવે તો બેસાડજો.
ते आले तर बसवून घ्या.
If he comes, ask him to wait.
(If they come, ask them to wait.)

किसी को भेजकर उन्हें बुलाओ.
Kisee ko bhaijker nhen bulaao.
कोई ने मोकलीने एने बोलावो.
कुणाला तरी पाठवून त्यांना बोलवा.
Send someone to call him (them).

आप नहीं जानते ?
Aap naheen jaantay ?
तमने खबर नथी ? तमे जाणता नथी ?
आपण जाणत नाही ? आपल्याला माहीत नाही ?
Don't you know ?

क्या फ़ायदा ?
Kya fayaada ?
शो फायदो ?
काय फायदा ?
What's the use ?

सुनिये तो.
Suniye to.
सांभळो तो.
ऐका तर खरे. ऐकून तर घ्या.
Just listen.

पंखा चला दो.
Pankhaa chalaa do.
पंखो चलावो.
पंखा चालू करा.
Switch on the fan.

मैं अभी आता हूँ.
Men abhee aata hun.
हुं हमणां आवुं छु.
मी आता येतो.
I am coming right away.   Just coming.

अभी आया.
Abhee aaya.
हमणां आव्यो.
हा आलोच.
(I'm) coming just now.

तैयार रहना.
Talyaar rahana.
तैयार रहेजो.
तयार रहा.
Be ready.

दीया जला दो.
Deeya jalaa do.
दीवो सळगावो.
दिवा लावा.
Light the lamp.

उनकी ख़बर रखना.
Unkee khabar rakhana.
तेमनी खबर (संभाळ) राखजो.
त्यांच्यावर लक्ष असू द्या.
Take care of him (them).

वे सो रहे हैं.
Way so rahe hain.
तेओ सुता छे.
ते झोपने आहेत.
He is asleep.   They are asleep

जरा इन्हें उठाइये.
Zaraa inhen uthaiye.
जरा आमने जगाडो.
ह्याना जरा उठवा.
Please wake him (them) up.

आते हैं.
Aatay hain.
आवे छे.
येत आहेत.
He is coming.   They ary coming.

आते होंगे.
Aatay hongay.
आवता हशे.
येत असतील.
He (They) might be coming.

कल मिलेंगे.
Kal milengay.
काले मळशुं
उद्या भेटू.
We shall meet tomorrow.   See you tomorrow.

पत्र लिखना.
Patra likhna.
पत्र लखजो.
पत्र लिहा.
Write to me.   Hope to hear from you.

उत्तर दीजिए.
Uttar deejiye.
जवाब आपो.
उत्तर द्या.
Please give reply.

जरा यहाँ आना.
Zaraa yahan aana.
जरा अहीं आवजो. जरा आम आवजो.
जरा इकडे या.
Please come here.

तुम ही जाओ.
Tum hee jaao.
तमेज जाव.
तुम्हीच जा.
You go (yourself).

तुम वहीं रहना.
Tum waheen rahna.
तमे त्यां ज रहेजो.
तुम्ही तेथेच राहा.
You stay there.

सुरेन्द्र, यहाँ आओ.
Surendra, yahan aao.
सुरेन्द्र, अहीं आवो.
सुरेन्द्र, इकडे ये.
Surendra, come here.

जी, आया.
Jee, aaya.
जी, आव्यो.
हो, आलो.
Coming, sir (or madam).

फूल मत तोड़ो.
Phool mat todo.
फूल ना तोड़ो.
फुले तोडू नका.
Don't pluck the flowers.

खेलना बंद करो.
Khailna band karo.
रमवानु (रमत) बंध करो.
खेलणे बंद करा.
Stop playing.

धूप में मत फिरो.
Dhoop men mat phiro.
तडकामां फरो नहीं.
उन्हात फिरू नका.
Don't go out in the sun.

अपना काम करो.
Apna kaam karo.
तमे तमारूं काम करो.
आपले काम करा.
Please mind your business.

जरा सब्र करो.
Zaraa sabr karo.
जरा सबूर करो. जरा थोभी जाओ.
जरा धीर धरा.
Have a little patience.

बीच में मत बोलो.
Beech men mat bolo.
वचमां बोलो नहीं.
मध्ये बोलू नका.
Don't interrupt.

बड़ों का अदब करो.
Bado ka adab karo.
मोटांने मान आपो.
वडिलांचा मान ठेवा.
Respect your elders.

कल इतवार है.
Kal Itwaar hai.
काले रविवार छे.
उद्या रविवार आहे.
Tomorrow is Sunday.

कल छुट्टी का दिन है. कल छुट्टी है.
Kal chhuttee ka din hai.   Kal chhuttee hai.
आवती काले रजा छे.
उद्या रजा आहे. उद्या सुटीचा दिवस आहे.
Tomorrow is a holiday.

क्या आज छुट्टी है ?
Kya aaj chhuttee hai ?
शुं आजे रजा छे ?
आज रजा (सुटी) आहे काय ?
Is it a holiday today ?

तुम्हें मालूम है ?
Tumhen maaloom hai ?
तमने खबर छे ?
तुम्हाला माहीत आहे ?
Do you know ?

कुछ परवा नहीं.
Kuchh parwa nahin.
कंई परवा नहीं.
काही हरकत नाही.
Never mind.   It doesn't matter.

बस, रहने दीजिये.
Bas, rahne, deejiye.
बस, रहेवा दो.
पुरे, राहू द्या.
Enough.   Let it be.

बहुत हो गया.
Bahut ho gayaa.
બહુ થયું.
अति झाले.
It is more than enough.

मुझे जाने दो.
Mujhe jaanay do.
મને જવા દો.
मला जाऊं द्या.
Let me go.

जल्दी क्या है ?
Jaldee kya hai ?
ઉતાવળ શી છે ? શી ઉતાવળ છે ?
घाई काय आहे ?
What is the hurry ?

खाना खाकर चलेंगे.
Khaano kha kar chalengay.
જમીને પછી જઈશું
जेवून जाऊ.
We shall go after meals.

पानी-वानी पी लो.
Paani-waani pee lo.
પાણી-બાણી પી લો.
पाणी-बिणी प्या.
Have some water.

मजाक मत करो.
Mazaaq mat karo.
मश्करी ना (नहीं) करो.
थट्टा करू नको.
Don't fool me.

अभी मत जाना.
Abhee mat jaana.
हमणां जता नहीं.
आता जाऊ नका.
Don't go just now.

गहरे पानी में न जाओ.
Gaharay paani men na jaao.
ऊंडा पाणीमां न जाओ.
खोल पाण्यात जाऊ नका.
Don't get into deep water.

गाड़ी धीरे चलाओ.
Gaadi dheeray chalaao.
गाडी धीरे हांको.
गाडी सावकाश चालवा.
Drive slowly.

आप दोनों आना.
Aap dono aana.
तमे बन्ने आवजो.
आपण दोघे यां.
Both of you may come.

वह. नहीं आएगा.
Wuh nahin aayega.
ते नहीं आवे.
तो येणार नाही.
He won't come.

क्या कारण (वजह) है ?
Kya kaaran (wajah) hai ?
कारण शुं छे ? शुं कारण छे ?
काय कारण आहे ? का ?
What is the reason ? Why ?

मैं नहीं जानता. मुझे नहीं मालूम.
Men nahin jaanata. Mujhe nahin maaloom.
हुं नथी जाणतो.
मला नाहीं ठाऊक. मला नाही माहीत.
I don't know

कोई बात नहीं.
Koi baat nahin.
कांई हरकत नहीं.
काही हरकत नाही.
It doesn't matter.

एक लिफ़ाफ़ा दीजिए.
Aik lifaafa deejiye.
एक परोबीडियुं आपो.
एक लिफाफा (पाकीट) द्या.
Please give me an envelope.

वह जरूर आएगा.
Wuh zaroor aayega.
ते जरूर आवशे.
तो जरूर येईल.
He will surely come.

यह बात नहीं.
Yeh baat nahin.
बात एम नथी.
असे काही नाही.
It is not so.

शोर मत मचाओ.
Shoar mat machaao.
अवाज नहीं करो.
गोंगाट करू नका.
Don't make any noise.

एक तरफ़ हो जाओ.
Aik taraf ho jaao.
एक बाजु थई जाओ.
एका बाजूला व्हा.
Move aside.

तुम जाओगे नहीं ?
Tum jaaogay nahin ?
तमे जशो नहीं ? तमे नहीं जाब ?
तुम्ही जाणार नाही ?
Won't you go ?

जा तो रहा हूँ.
Jaa to raha hun.
जई तो रह्यो छु
जातो तर आहे.
I *am* going.

जल्दी वापस आना.
Jaldi waapas aana.
जल्दी पाछा आवजो.
लबकर परत या
Come back soon.

मुझे घर जाना है.
Mujhe ghar jaana hai.
मारे घेर जवुं छे.
मला घरी जावयाचे आहे.
I have to go home.   I want to go home.

फिर कभी आना.
Phir kabhi aana.
फरी कोईवार आवजो.
पुन: कधीतरी या.
Come some other time.

अच्छी बात है. .
Achchhi baat hai.
सारु
ठीक आहे.
All right.   Very well.

सोच समझकर बोलो.
Soach samajh kar bolo.
विचारींने बोलो.
विचार करून बोला.
Think before you speak.

इसे लिख लो.
Ise likh lo.
आ लखी लो.
हे .लिहून घ्या.
Note (Write) this down.   Take this down.

आप बोल चुके ?
Aap boal chuke ?
आप बोली रह्या ?
आपले बोलणे संपले ?
Have you finished speaking ?

क्या मामला है ?
Kya maamla hai ?
शी वात छे ?
काय भानगड आहे ?
What is the matter ?

क्या गड़बड़ है ?
Kya gadbad hai ?
शी गरबड छे ?
काय गडबड आहे ?
What is the trouble ?

क्या झगड़ा है ?
Kya jhagda hai ?
शो झगडो छे ?
काय भांडण आहे ?
What is the quarrel about ?

दर्पण किसने तोड़ा है ?
Darpan kisne toda hai ?
दर्पण कोने तोड्यु छे ?
आरसा कोणी फोडला ?
Who has broken this mirror ?

आप नाराज़ हो गये ?
Aap naaraz ho gaye ?
तमे नाराज थई गया ? नाराज थया ?
तुम्ही नाखूष झालात ?
Are you angry (annoyed) ?

मैं तो मज़ाक कर रहा था.
Men to mazaaq kar raha tha.
हुं तो मश्करी करतो हतो.
मी तर गंमत (थट्टा) करीत होतो.
I was just joking.

तुमको उससे मज़ाक़ नहीं करना चाहिए.
Tumko usse mazaaq nahin karna chaahiye.
तमारे एनी मश्करी नहीं करवी जोईअे.
तू त्यांची चेष्टा करता कामा नये.
You should not joke with (make fun of) him.

दस्तखत कीजिये.
Dastkhat keejiye.
सही करो.
सही करा.
Please sign here. Please put your signature here.

हिचकिचाते क्यों हो ?
Hichkichcatay kyon ho ?
अचकाव छो केम ? केम अचकाव छो ?
आढेवेढे का घेता ?
Why do you hesitate ?

दा़खिला बन्द हो गया.
Daakhila band ho gaya.
प्रवेश बंध थई गयो.
प्रवेश बंद झाला.
Admission is closed.

कोई हर्ज नहीं.
Koi harj nahin.
कांई वांधो नथी. कोई हरकत नथी.
काही हरफत नाही.
It does not matter.

फिक्र मत करो.
Fikr mat karo.
चिंता न करो. चिंता करो नहीं.
काळजी नका करू.
Don't worry.

बेफ़िक्र राहय.

Bay-fikr rahiye.

बेफिकर रहो. चिंता नहीं करो.

निश्चिंत राहा.

Rest assured.

घबराओ मत. घबराते क्यों हो ?

Ghabraao mat.   Ghabraate kyon ho ?

गभराओ नहीं. शा माटे गभराओ छो ?

घाबरू नका. घाबरता का ?

Don't get nervous.

Why are you getting nervous ?

यह नामुमकिन है.

Yeh naamumkin hai.

आ असंभवित छे.

हे अशक्य आहे.

This is impossible.

एक काम करोगे ?

Aik kaam karogay ?

एक काम करशो ?

एक काम कराल ?

Will you do one thing ?

मैं तुम्हें खुश कर दूँगा.

Men tumhen khush kar doonga.

हुं तमने राजी करी दईश.

मी तुम्हाला खूष करीन.

I will satisfy you.

लानत भेजो.
Laanat bhejo.
धिक्कार बरसाओ. फिटकार करो. मूको ने हवे.
धिक्कार असो. सोडून द्या ना.
Damn it.   Down with it.

जैसी आपकी मर्ज़ी.
Jesi aap ki marzee.
जेवी तमारी मरज़ी.
जशी आपली मर्ज़ी.
As you like.

आइयेगा.
Aaiyega.
आवजो.
यावे.
Please come again.   Good-bye.

आते रहना. आते रहियेगा.
Aatay rahna.   Aatay rahiyega.
आवता रहेजो.
येत जा. येत जाव.
Do come often.   See me sometimes.

3. घरेलू (2) [Domestic (2)]

मेरे खत का जवाब आ गया.
Meray khat ka jawaab aa gaya.
મારા પત્રનો જવાબ આવી ગયો.
माझ्या पत्राचे उत्तर आले.
I have received a reply to my letter.

मेरे पत्र का कोई उत्तर नहीं आया.
Meray patra ka koi uttar nahin aaya.
મારા કાગળનો કોઈ જવાબ આવ્યો નથી.
माझ्या पत्राचे काही उत्तर आले नाही.
I have not received a reply to my letter.

इस किताब की छपाई सुन्दर है.
Is kitab ki chhapaaee sundar hai.
આ ચોપડીની છપાઈ સુન્દર છે.
या पुस्तकाची छपाई सुंदर आहे.
This book is well printed.

हिन्दी का सबसे अच्छा दैनिक पत्र कौन-सा है ?
Hindi ka sab se achchha denik patra kaunsa hai?
હિંદીમાં સૌથી સારું દૈનિક છાપું કયું છે ?
सर्वात चांगले हिंदी दैनिक कोणते ?
Which is the best Hindi daily paper ?

आजकल आप क्या पढ़ रहे हैं ?
Aajkal aap kya padh rahe hain ?
आज-कल तमे शुं वांचो छो ?
हल्ली आपण काय वाचता ?
What are you reading these days ?

मुझसे वह किताब खो गई.
Mujhse wuh kitab kho gayi.
माराथी ते चोपड़ी खोवाई गई.
माझ्याकडून ते पुस्तक हरवले.
I have lost that book.

मैं तुम्हारे लिये एक नई चीज़ लाया हूँ.
Men tumhaare liye aik nayee cheez laaya hun.
हुं तमारे माटे एक नवी चीज लाव्यो छुं.
मी तुमच्यासाठी एक नवीन वस्तु आणली आहे.
I have brought something new for you.

मैं उसे तुम्हारे पास भेज दूँगा.
Men usay tumhare paas bhej doonga.
हुं तेने तमारी पासे मोकली दईश.
मी त्याला तुमच्याकडे पाठवून देईन.
I shall send him to you.

आप के बिना कुछ नहीं हो सकता.
Aap ke bina kuchh nahin ho sakta.
तमारा विना कंई थई शके नहीं.
आपल्याशिवाय काही होऊ शकत नाही.
Nothing can be done without you.

आप के गये बिना काम नहीं होगा.

Aap ke gaye bina kaam nahin hoga.

तमारा गया वगर काम नहीं थाय.

आपण गेल्याशिवाय काम होणार नाही.

Unless you go there, the work will never be done.

अब तुम जाओ, मुझे काम है.

Ab tum jaao, mujhe kaam hai.

हवे तमे जाओ, मारे काभ छे.

आता तुम्ही जा, मला काम आहे.

You may go now.   I have some work to do.

मुझे बहुत काम रहता है.

Mujhe bahut kaam rehta hai.

मारे गणुं काम रहे छे.

मला पुष्कळ काम असते.

I always have a lot of work to do.

मुझसे यह काम अकेले न होगा.

Mujhse yeh kaam akelay na hoga.

माराथी आ काम एकला नहीं थाय.

माझ्या एकट्याच्याने हे काम होणार नाही.

I will not be able to do this work alone.

यह तो मैं आसानी से कर सकता हूँ.

Yeh to men aasaani se kar sakta hun.

आ तो हुं सहेलाईथी करी शकुं छु.

हें तर मी सहज करू शकतो.

I can do this quite easily.

उसने आने का वादा किया है.
Usne aanay ka waada kiya hai.

तेणे आववानो वायदो कर्यो छे.

त्याने येण्याचे वचन दिले आहे.

He has promised to come.

यह उसके बस की बात नहीं.
Yeh uske bas ki baat nahin.

आ तेना हाथनी वात नथी.

ही त्याच्या हातची गोष्ट नव्हे.

It is beyond his capacity.

यह उसके बस का काम नहीं.
Yeh uske bas ka kaam nahin.

आ एना गजानुं काम नथी.

ही त्याच्या आवाक्यातील गोष्ट नाही.

This work is beyond his ability.

ग्यारह बजे तक हम खाना खा चुकेंगे.
Gyaarah baje tak ham khaana kha chukengay.

अग्यार वाग्ये अमे जमी लईशुं.

अकरा वाजेपर्यंत आम्ही जेऊन घेऊ.

We will have finished our meal by eleven o'clock.

कल मैं तुम्हारे यहाँ गया, मगर तुम बाहर गये हुए थे.
Kal men tumhaare yahan gaya, magar tum baahar gaye huye thay.

काले हुं तमारे त्यां आव्यो, पण तमे बहार गया हता.

काल मी तुमच्याकडे गेलो होतो, पण तुम्ही बाहेर गेला होता.

I went to your house yesterday, but you had gone out.

बना बनाया काम बिगड़ गया.
Bana banaya kaam bigad gaya.
पार पडेलुं काम बगडी गयुं.
पूर्ण झालेले काम बिघडले.
What was done has been undone.

मेरे पहुँचने के पहले ही वह घर से चल दिये थे.
Mere pahunchne ke pahle hi wuh ghar se chal diye thay.
मारा पहोंच्या पहेलां तेओ घेरथी नीकळी चुक्या हता.
मी पोहोचण्याच्या पूर्वींच ते घरातून निघून गेले होते.
He had left his home, before I arrived.

फ़िक्र की कोई बात नहीं.
Fikr ki koi baat nahin.
चिंतानुं कंई कारण नथी.
काळजी करण्याचे काही कारण नाही.
There is no need to worry.

बड़े अफ़सोस की बात है.
Baday afsoas ki baat hai.
घणा खेदनी वात छे.
मोठ्या दुःखाची गोष्ट आहे.
It's a pity.

मैंने अपना इरादा बदल दिया.
Menay apna iraada badal diya.
में मारो विचार बदली नांख्यो.
मी माझा बेत बदलला.
I have changed my mind.

मेरा दिल यहाँ नहीं लगता.
Mera dil yahan nahin lagta.
माझ मन अहीं चोंटतुं नथी.
माझे मन ग्रेथे लागत नाही.
I am not happy here.

यहाँ रहते रहते मेरी तबियत ऊब गयी है.
Yahan rahte rahte meri tabiyat oob gayee hai.
अहीं रहीने हुं कटाळी गयो छुं.
ह्या जागेला माझे मन विटले आहे.
I am fed up with this place.

मुझे साफ़ और शान्त जगह चाहिए.
Mujhe saaf aur shaant jagah chahiye.
मारे साफ अने शांत जग्या जोईए.
मला स्वच्छ व शांत जागा पाहिजे.
I want a clean and quiet place.

मेरी भी यही कठिनाई है.
Meri bhi yahi kathinayee hai.
मारे पण आज मुश्केली छे.
माझी सुद्धा हीच अडचण आहे.
I have the same difficulty.

मैंने तुमसे पहले ही कह दिया था.
Mene tumse pahile hi kah diya tha.
में तुमने पहलेथी ज कह्यं हतुं.
मी तुम्हाला आधीच सांगितले होते.
I had told you beforehand.

उसने सिगरेट पीना छोड़ दिया.

Usne sigret peena chhod diya.

एणे सिगरेट पीवी छोडी दीधी.

त्याने सिगरेट ओढणे सोडून दिले.

He has given up smoking.

हमें यह जानकर बहुत खुशी हुई.

Hamen yeh jaankar bahut khushi hui.

अमने ए जाणीने बहु खुशी थई.

आम्हाला हे ऐकून फार आनंद झाला.

We are very pleased to hear this.

आपकी बात सच निकली.

Aap ki baat sach niklee.

तमारी बात साची नीकली.

आपले म्हणणे खरे ठरले.

What you had said proved to be right.

आपकी तरकीब काम कर गई.

Aap ki tarkeeb kaam kar gayee

तमारी युक्ति सफळ थई.

आपल्या युक्तीने काम केले.

Your trick worked.

आपने तो कमाल कर दिया !

Aapne to kamaal kar diya !

तमें तो कमाल करी !

आपण तर कमाल केली !

You acted splendidly !

तुमसे इतनी दूर पैदल नहीं चला जायेगा.
Tum so itnee door pedal nahin chala jayega.
તભારાથી આટલુ દૂર પગે નહીં ચલાય.
तुमच्याने एवढे लांब पायी चालवणार नाही.
You will not be able to walk so far.

वे कल वापस जा रहे हैं.
Way kal waapas ja rahe hain.
તેઓ કાલે પાછા જઈ રહ્યા છે.
ते उद्या परत जाणार आहेत.
They are returning tomorrow.

मैं वहाँ कभी नहीं गया.
Men wahan kabhi nahin gaya.
હું ત્યાં કદી ગયો નથી.
मी तेथे कधीच गेलो नाही.
I have never been there.

मेरा वहाँ जाना मुनासिब नहीं है.
Maira wahan jaana munaasib nahin hai.
મારું ત્યાં જવું યોગ્ય નથી.
माझे तेथे जाणे योग्य नाही.
It is not proper for me to go there.

मुझे वहाँ जाने का ख्याल नहीं रहा.
Mujhe wahan jane ka khyal nahin raha.
મને ત્યાં જવાનો ખ્યાલ નહીં રહ્યો.
मला तेथे जाण्याची आठवण राहिली नाही.
I did not remember to go there.
I forgot to go there.

आप वहाँ कितने दिन ठहरेंगे ?

Aap wahan kitne din thaharengay ?

तमे त्यां केटला दिवस रोकाशो ?

आपण तेथे किती दिवस राहाल ?

How long will you stay there ?

वहाँ दो महीने ठहरूँगा.

Wahaan do maheenay thaharoonga.

त्यां बे महीना रोकाईश.

मी तेथे दोन महिने राहिन.

I shall stay there for two months.

मैं दिवाली पर घर जा रहा हूँ.

Men Diwali par ghar jaa raha hun.

हुं दिवाळी पर घेर जाउं छुं.

भी दिवाळीला घरी जाणार आहें.

I am going home for Diwali.

मैं दो दिन से छुट्टी पर हूँ.

Men do din se chhutti par hun.

हुं बे दिवसथी रजा पर छुं.

मी दोन दिवसांपासून रजेवर आहें.

I am on leave for the last two days.

आप इन छुट्टियों में कहाँ जायेंगे ?

Aap in chhuttiyon men kahan jayengay ?

तमे आ रजाओमां क्यां जशो ?

आपण या सुट्टीत कोठे जाणार ?

Where will you be going during these holidays

रविवार को हम लोग सैर करने जा रहे हैं.
Ravivar ko ham loag ser karne jaa rahay hain.
रविवारे अमे लोको फरवा जवाना छीए.(उजाणी करवा).
रविवारी आम्ही सहलीला जाणार आहोत.
We are going for a picnic on Sunday.

वादा करो कि जरूर आओगे.
Waada karo ki zaroor aaogay.
वचन आपो के जरूर आवीशो.
खात्रीने याल असे वचन द्या.
Promise that you will definitely come.

मैं आने की भरसक कोशिश करूँगा.
Men aanay ki bharsak koshish karoonga.
हुं आववानी पूरी कोशिश करीश.
मी येण्याचा पूर्ण प्रयत्न करीन.
I will try my level best to come.
I'll strive my best to come.

मैं उसे वर्षों से जानता हूँ.
Men usay varshon se jaanata hun.
हुं तेने वरसोथी जाणु छु.
मी त्याला पुष्कळ वर्षांपासून ओळखतो.
I know him for years.

मुझे उस पर पूरा भरोसा है.
Mujhe uspar poora bharosa hai.
मने तेना पर पूरो भरोसो छे.
माझा त्याच्यावर पूर्ण विश्वास आहे.
I have full faith in him.

वह सरकारी मुलाज़िम है।
Wuh sarkaari mulaazim hai.
ते सरकारी नोकर छे.
तो सरकारी नोकर आहे.
He is a Government servant.

मेरी उससे जान पहचान नहीं है।
Meri us-se jaan pehchaan nahin hai.
मारे तेनी साथे ओळखाण नथी.
माझी आणि त्याची ओळख नाही.
I don't know him.   We don't know each other.

मेरा उससे कोई वास्ता (सम्बन्ध) नहीं।
Mera us-se koi waasta (sambandh) nahin.
मारे एनी साथे कोई संबंध नथी.
माझा त्याच्याशी काही संबंध नाही.
I have no connection with him.

मेरे दस्तखत की ज़रूरत नहीं है।
Merey dastkhat ki zaroorat nahin hai.
मारी सहीनी जरूर नथी.
माझ्या सहीची जरूरी नाही.
My signature is not necessary.

मैं इस पर अपने दस्तखत नहीं कर सकता।
Men ispar apne dastkhat nahin kar sakta.
हुं आना पर मारी सही नहीं करी शकुं.
मी याच्यावर सही करू शकत नाही.
I can't sign this.

यह दोनों के फ़ायदे की बात है.
Yeh dono ke faayede ki baat hai.
आ બન્નેના ફાયદાની વાત છે.
ही दोघांच्या फायद्याची गोष्ट आहे.
This is for our mutual benefit.

ऐसा अच्छा मौक़ा फिर हाथ नहीं आयेगा.
Esa achchha mauqa phir haath nahin aayegaa.
આવી સારી તક ફરી હાથ નહીં આવે.
अशी चांगली संधी पुनः मिळणार नाही.
Such a good opportunity will not occur again.

अपने दिमाग़ से काम लो.
Apne dimaag se kaam lo.
પોતાની બુદ્ધિથી કામ કરો.
स्वतःच्या बुद्धीने (डोक्याने) काम करा.
Do your work intelligently.
Do your work mindfully.

अपना अपना काम करो.
Apna apna kaam karo.
પોતપોતાનું કામ કરો.
आपापलें काम करा.
Do your own work.

आप रहने दीजिये, मैं करता हूँ.
Aap rahane deejiye, men karta hun.
તમે રહેવા દો, હું કરૂ છુ.
आपण राहू द्या, मी करता.
Let it be, I will do it.

वह कुछ न कुछ काम करती रहती है.
Wuh kuchh na kuchh kaam karti rahati hai.
તે કંઈ ન કંઈ કામ કરતી જ હોય છે.
तो काही न-काही काम करीतच राहते.
She is always doing something or the other.

अगर वह मेहनत करता तो पास होता.
Agar wuh mehnat karte to pass hota.
જો તે મહેનત કરત તો પાસ થઈ જાત.
जर त्याने मेहनत केली असती तर तो पास झाला असता.
If he had worked hard, he would have passed.

मुझे उसका नाम याद नहीं आ रहा.
Mujhe uska nam yaad nahin aa raha.
મને એનુ નામ યાદ નથી આવતું.
मला त्याचे नाव आठवत नाही.
I don't remember his name.

आप तो पहचाने नहीं जाते.
Aap to pehchaane nahin jaatay.
તમે તો ઓળખાતા પણ નથી.
आपल्याला ओळखता सुद्धा येत नाही.
You have changed beyond recognition.
You are beyond recognition.

मैं एक नौकर की तलाश में हूँ.
Men aik naukar ki talaash men hun.
હું એક નોકરની તપાસમાં છું.
मी एका नोकराच्या शोधात आहे.
I am looking for a servant.

आज मैं दफ्तर नहीं जाऊँगा.
Aaj men daftar nahin jaoonga.
आजे हुं ऑफिसमां नहीं जाउं.
आज भी कामावर जाणार नाही.
I am not going to the office to-day.

यहाँ की आबादी कितनी है ?
Yahan ki aabaadi kitni hai ?
अहींनी वस्ती केटली छे ?
येथीली लोकसंख्या (वस्ती) किती आहे ?
What is the population of this place ?

उनकी बदली कानपुर हो गई.
Unki badli Kanpur ho gayee.
तेमनी बदली कानपूर थई.
त्यांची बदली कानपूरला झाली.
He has been transferred to Kanpur.

क्या तुम कल वहाँ गये थे ?
Kya tum kal wahan gaye thay ?
शुं काले तमे त्यां गया हता ?
तुम्ही काल तेथे गेला होता का ?
Did you go there yesterday ?

नहीं, मैं नहीं जा सका.
Nahin, men nahin jaa saka.
ना, हुं न जई शक्यो.
नाही, मी जाऊ शकलो नाही.
No, I couldn't go.

उस रोज़ मैं बाहर **गया** हुआ था.
Us rooz men baahar gaya hua tha.
ते दिवसे हुं बहार गयो हेतो.
त्या दिवशी मी बाहेर गेलो होतो.
I had gone out that day.

आजे सुबह मेरी आँख देर से खुली.
Aaj subah meri aankh dair se khuli.
आज सवारे मारी आंख मोडी खुली.
आज सकाळी मी उशिरा जागा झालो.
I woke up late this morning.

आप अभी तक जाग रहे हैं ?
Aap abhi tak jaag rahe hain ?
तमे हजी सुधी जागो छो ?
आपण अजून जागे आहात ?
You are still awake ?

मैं ज़रा आराम कर लूँ.
Men zara aaraam kar loon.
हुं जरा आराम करी लउं.
मी जरा विश्रांति घेतो.
I will rest for a while.

क्या ठंडी ठंडी हवा आ रही है !
Kya thandi thandi hawa aa rahi hai !
केवी ठंडी ठंडी हवा वाई रही छे !
किती गार वारा वाहत आहे !
What a cool breeze !

आपने मुझे जगा क्यों नहीं लिया ?
Aapne mujhe jaga kyon nahin liya.
तमे .मने जगाड्यो केम नहीं ?
आपण मला का नाही उठविले ?
Why did you not wake me up ?

मैंने आपको जगाना मुनासिब नहीं समझा.
Mene aapko jagaana munaasib nahin samjha.
तमने जगाडवुं मने योग्य लाग्युं नहीं.
आपल्याला उठविणे मला योग्य वाटले नाही.
I did not think it proper to wake you up.

यह बिलकुल ठीक है.
Yeh bilkul theek hai.
ए तद्दन बराबर छे.
हे अगदी बरोबर आहे.
This is quite right.

उनका खत आया है.
Unka khat aaya hai.
तेमनो पत्र आव्यो छे.
त्यांचे पत्र आले आहे.
His letter has come.

मेरी अर्जी मंजूर हो गयी.
Meri arzee manzoor ho gayee.
मारी अरजी मंजूर थई गई.
माझा अर्ज मंजूर झाला.
My application has been accepted.

मुझे एक चिट्ठी लिखनी है.
Mujhe aik chitthi likhni hai.
मारे एक पत्र लखवो छे.
मला एक पत्र लिहावयाचे आहे.
I have to write a letter.

उसे छुट्टी नहीं मिली.
Usay chhuttee nahin mili.
तेने रजा ना मळी.
त्याला रजा मिळाली नाही.
He did not get leave.

मैं अभी तैयार होता हूँ.
Men abhi tayyar hota hun.
हुं हमणां ज तैयार थाउं छुं.
मी आताच तयार होतो.
I shall be ready in a moment.

तुमने बड़ी देर लगाई.
Tumne badi dair lagaayee.
तमे घणी वार लगांडी.
तुम्ही फार वेळ लावला.
You have taken too much time.

वे अभी नहीं आये.
Way abhi nahin aaye.
तेओ हजी आव्या नहीं.
ते अजून आले नाहीत.
He hasn't come yet.

वे अब आते ही होंगे.
Way ab aatay hee honge.
तेओ हवे आवदा ज हशे.
ते एवढ्यात येतच असतील.
He must be on his way.

वे आने ही वाले हैं.
Way anne hi waale hain.
तेओ आवता ज हशे.
ते येणारच आहेत.
He is about to come.

उनके घर का पता क्या है ?
Unke ghar ka pata kya hai ?
तेमना घरनुं सरनामुं शुं छे ?
त्यांच्या घराचा पत्ता काय आहे ?
What is his residential address ?

क्या आपको उनका पता मालूम है ?
Kya aapko unka pata maaloom hai ?
शुं तमने तेमना सरनामानी खबर छे ?
आपल्याला त्यांचा पता माहीत आहे काय ?
Do you know his address ?

तुम यहाँ कैसे ?
Tum yahan kesay ?
तुं अहीं क्यांथी ?
तुम्ही येथे कसे ?
How is it that you are here ?

जरूर कुछ बात है.

Zaroor kutchh baat hai.

जरूर कंईक कारण छे.

जरूर काही तरी भानगड आहे.

There must be a snag (hitch) son.ewhere.

हम आज जा रहे हैं.

Ham aaj ja rahe hain.

अमे आजे जईए छीए.

आम्ही आज जाणार आहोत.

We are going today.

आप क्या कहते हैं ?

Aap kya kahte hain.

तमे शुं कहो छो ?

आपण काय म्हणता ?

What do you say ?

आज कौन-सी तारीख है ?

Aaj kaunsi tareekh hai ?

आजे कई तारीख छे ?

आज कोणती तारीख आहे ?

What is the date today ?

आज इक्कीस मार्च है.

Aaj ikkees March hai.

आजे २१ मार्च छे.

आज अकवीस मार्च आहे.

Today is the twenty-first of March.

देखो, बच्चा क्यों रोता है.
Dekho, bachchaa kyon rota hai.
जुओ,.बाळक केम रडे छे.
बघा, मूल का रडत आहे.
Go and see why the child is crying.

वह आप से डरता है.
Wuh aapse darta hai.
ते तमाराथी डरे छे.
तो तुम्हाला भितो आहे.
He is afraid of you.

चोट तो नहीं आई ?
Choat to nahin aayee ?
तमने वाग्युं तो नथी ने ?
कुठे लागले तर नाही ?
Did you get hurt ?

आधा भाग उसे दो.
Aadha bhaag usay do.
अडधो भाग एने आपो.
अर्धा भाग त्याला (तिला) द्या.
Give him (her) half.

यह बहुत ज्यादा है.
Yeh bahut zyaada hai.
आ घणुं वधारे छे.
हे फारच जास्त आहे.
This is too much.

मुझे इसकी परवाह नहीं.
Mujhe iski parwah nahin.
मने एनी परवा नथी.
मला याची पर्वा नाही.
I don't care for this.

मैं सोचकर जवाब दूँगा.
Men soach kar jawaab doonga.
हुं विचार करीने जवाब आपीश.
मी विचार करून उत्तर देईन.
I shall think it over and give you a reply.

मैं पूछकर बताऊँगा.
Men poochhkar bataaoonga.
हुं पूछीने जणावीश.
मी विचारून सांगेन.
I shall inquire and let you know.

मुझे काम करने दो.
Mujhe kaam karne do.
मने काम करवा दो.
मला काम करू द्या.
Let me work.

जरा देखने तो दो.
Zaraa daikhne to do.
जरा जोवा तो दो.
जरा पाहू तरी द्या.
Please let me have a look.

अब आप जा सकते हैं.
Ab aap ja sakte hain.
હવે તમે જઈ શકો છો.
आतां आपण जाऊ शकता.
You may go now.

उन्हें आराम करने दीजिए.
Unhen aaraam karne deejiye.
એમને આરામ કરવા દો.
त्यांना विश्रांति घेऊ द्या.
Let him rest.

मैं फिर कभी आऊँगा.
Men phir kabhi aaoonga.
હું ફરી કોઈ વાર આવીશ.
मी पुन्हा कधी तरी येईन.
I will come some other time.

सब कुछ तैयार है.
Sab kutchh taiyyar hai.
બધું તૈયાર છે.
सर्व काही तयार आहे.
Everything is ready.

बड़ी खुशी की बात है.
Badi khushee ki baat hai.
ઘણી ખુશીની વાત છે.
मोठ्या आनंदाची गोष्ट आहे.
It is a matter of great joy.

मुझे नींद आ रही है.
Mujhe neend aa rahi hai.
मने ऊंध आवे छे.
मला झोप येत आहे.
I am feeling sleepy.

बस, अब सो जाओ.
Bas, ab so jaao.
बस, हवे सूई जाओ.
पुरे, आता झोपा.
Go and sleep now.

रात खूब नींद आई.
Raat khoob neend aayee.
रात्रे खूब ऊंध आवी.
रात्रीं गाढ झोप लागली.
I had a sound sleep last night.

मैं तुम्हें वहीं मिलूंगा.
Men tumhen waheen miloonga.
हुं तमने त्यां ज मळीश.
मी तुम्हांला तेथेंच भेटेन.
I shall meet you there.

आज मैं उनसे मिलूंगा.
Aaj men unse miloonga.
आजे हुं तेमने मळीश.
आज मी त्यांना भेटेन.
I shall meet him today.

मैं उनसे कल मिला था.

Men unse kal mila tha.

हुं एमने काले मळ्यो हतो.

मी त्यांना काल भेटल होतों.

I met him yesterday.

तुम घर पर नहीं थे.

Tum ghar par nahin thay.

तमे घरमां नहता.

तुम्ही घरी नव्हतां.

You were not at home.

मुझे उनके आने की खबर पहुँचा देना.

Mujhe unke aanay ki khabar pahuncha dena.

मने तेमना आववानी खबर पहोंचाडजो.

मला ते आल्याचे कळवा.

Please let me know when he comes.

वे आवें तो मुझे खबर करना.

Way aaven to mujhe khabar karna.

तेओ आवे तो मने खबर आपजो.

ते आले तर मला कळवा.

Please inform me of his arrival.

आपके कमरे में ताला लगा हुआ था.

Aap ke kamray men taala laga hua tha.

तमारा ओरडाने ताळुं हतुं.

आपल्या खोलीला कुलूप होते.

Your room was locked.

आपका कहना ठीक है.
Aapka kahna theek hei.
तमारुं कहेवुं बराबर छे.
आपले म्हणणे बरोबर आहे.
You are right.

अन्दर कोई नहीं है.
Andar koi nahin hai.
अन्दर कोई नथी.
आत कोणी नाही.
There is no one inside.

वह तो कभी का चला गया.
Wuh to kabhi ka chala gaya.
ए तो क्यारनो चाल्यो गयो.
तो तर केव्हाच निघून गेला.
He left long before.

शायद वह कल आयेगा.
Shaayad wuh kal aayega.
कदाच ए काले आवशे.
कदाचित् तो उद्या येईल.
Perhaps he may come tomorrow.

वह घर पर होगा.
Wuh ghar par hoga.
ते घरमां हशे.
तो घरी असेल.
He will be in his home.

वे इस वक्त घर पर होंगे.
Way is waqt ghar par hongay.
तेओ आत्यारे घरमां हशे.
ते या वेळी घरी असतील.
They will be in their home at this time.

वे घर पर नहीं मिले.
Way ghar par nehin milay.
तेओ घरमां मळ्या नहीं.
ते घरी भेटले नाहीत.
They were not at home.

वे कहीं बाहर गये हैं.
Way kaheen baahar gaye hain.
तेओ क्यांक बहार गया छे.
ते कोठे बाहेर गेले आहेत.
They have gone out somewhere.

चलो अब घूमने चलें.
Chalo ab ghoomnay chalen.
चालो हवे फरवा जईए.
चला आता फिरायला जाऊ.
Come, let us go for a walk now.

4. घरेलू (3) [Domestic (3)]

आप हमारे यहाँ कब आयेंगे ?
Aap hamaaray yahaan kab aayengay ?
तमे अमारे त्यां क्यारे आवशो ?
आपण आमच्याकडे केव्हा याल ?
When will you come to us ?

आज शाम को हमारे यहाँ आइए.
Aaj shaam ko hamaaray yahaan aaiye.
आज सांजे अमारे त्यां आवजो.
आज संध्याकाळी आमच्याकडे या.
Please come to our place this evening.

फुर्सत मिली तो आऊँगा.
Fursat milee to aaoonga.
फुरसद मळशे तो आवीश.
सवड मिळाली तर येईन.
I will come if I find time.

कल न आ सका तो परसों आऊँगा.
Kal na aa sakaa to parson aaoonga.
काले ना आवी शकुं तो परम दिवसे आवीश.
उद्या येऊ शकलो नाही, तर परवा येईन.
If I cannot come tomorrow, I shall come
 the day after.

ऐसी बात नहीं कहते.
Esi baat nahin kahte.

आवी वात न थाय.

असं बोलू नये.

Such a thing is not talked.
It's not proper to talk this way.

मुझे इसका. बड़ा अफ़सोस है.
Mujhe iska bada afsoas hai.

मने आनो बहु खेद छे.

मला याबद्दल फार वाईट वाटते.

I am very sorry about this.

आप हमसे नाराज़ हैं क्या ?
Aap hamse naaraaz hain kya ?

तमे अमारा पर नाराज छो शुं ?

आपण माझ्यावर रागावलात का ?

Are you annoyed with me ?

न मालूम क्या कारण है.
Na maloom kya kaaran hai.

शुं कारण छे तेनी मने खबर नथी.

काय कारण आहे, ठाऊक नाही.

I don't know the reason

आप एक कृपा करेंगे ?
Aap aik krapa karengay ?

तमे एक महेरबानी करशो ?

आपण एक कृपा कराल ?

Will you do me a favour ?

बेशक.

Baishak.

जरूर, बेशक.

बेलाशक, जरूर.

Certainly. Undoubtedly.

वह अभी घर नहीं आये.

Wuh abhi ghar nahin aaye.

ते हजी घेर नथी आव्या.

ते अजून घरो नाही आले.

He hasn't come home yet.

अब क्या किया जाय ?

Ab kya kiya jaaye ?

हवे शुं करवुं ?

आता काय करावे ?

What is to be done now ?

कुछ तदबीर कीजिये.

Kuchh tadbeer keejiye.

कंईक युक्ति करोः

काही युक्ति काढा.

Find a way out.

यह सब झंझट छोड़िये.

Yeh sab jhanjhat chhodiye.

आ बधी माथाफोड छोडो.

ही सर्व डोकेफोड सोडून द्या.

Leave aside all this bothe

देखें, क्या होता है.
Daikhen, kya hota hai.
जुओ, शुं थाय छेते.
बघू, काय होते ते.
Let us see what happens.

मैंने उसे एक लम्बा पत्र लिखा है.
Mene usay aik lamba patra likha hai.
में तेने एक लांबो पत्र लख्यो छे.
मी त्याला एक लांबलचक पत्र लिहिले आहे.
I have written him a long letter.

जरा कागज़ पेंसिल देना.
Zara kaagaz pencil dena.
जरा कागद पेन्सिल आपजो.
जरा कागद-पेन्सिल द्या.
Please give me pencil and paper.

तुम यहाँ कब से बैठे हो ?
Tum yahaan kab se bethay ho ?
तमे अहीं क्यारना बेठा छो ?
तुम्ही येथे केव्हापासून बसला आहाव ?
Since when you are sitting here ?

मैं बहुत देर का आया हुआ हूँ.
Men bahut dair ka aaya hua hoon.
हुं तो घणीवारथी आव्यो छु.
मला येऊन बराच वेळ झाला.
I am here for a long time.

वह मेरे पास नहीं आया.
Wuh meray paas nahin aaya
ते मारी पासे आव्यो नहीं.
तो माझ्याकडे आला नाही.
He did not come to me.

तुम्हें वहाँ जरूर जाना चाहिये.
Tumhen wahan zaroor jaana chahiye.
तमारे त्यां जरूर जबुं जोईए.
तुम्हाला तेथे अवश्य जावयाला पाहिजे.
You must go there.

अच्छा हुआ तुम वहाँ नहीं गये.
Achchha hua tum wahaan nahin gaye.
सारुं थयुं के तमे त्यां नहीं गया.
तुम्ही तेथे गेला नाही हे छान झाले.
Thank goodness you didn't go there.
It's good that you have not gone there.

कह तो दिया मैं नहीं आता.
Kah to diya men nahin aata.
कही दीधुं के हुं नहीं आवुं.
सांगितले ना, की मी येत नाही.
I have already told (you) that I am not coming.

ऐसा नहीं हो सकता.
Esa nahin ho sakta.
एम नहीं थई शके.
असे होऊ शकत नाही.
It can't be so.

आप इसे अपने साथ ले जाइये.
Aap ise apne saath lay jaaiye.
तमे आने तमारी साथे लई जाओ.
आपण हे आपल्याबरोबर घेऊन जावे.
Please take this with you.

कोई कठिनाई हो तो पूछिये.
Koi kathinaayi ho to poochhiye.
कई मुश्केली होय तो पूछजो.
काही अडचण असेल तर विचारावे.
Ask (me) if there is any difficulty.

जिस चीज़ की ज़रूरत पड़े ले लेना.
Jis cheez ki zaroorat pade lay lena.
जे वस्तुनी जरूर पड़े ते लई लेजो.
ज्या वस्तूची आवश्यकता असेल ती घ्या.
Take whatever you need.

चलने दीजिये, बहुत देर हो गयी.
Chalne deejiye, bahut dair ho gayee
जवा दो, घणुं मोडुं थई गयुं.
जाऊ द्या, बराच उशीर झाला आहे.
Let it be, it's very very late.

मैं सुबह का घर से निकला हूँ.
Men subeh ka ghar se nikla hoon.
हुं सवारनो घेरथी नीकळयो छुं.
मी सकाळीच घराबाहेर पडलो आहे.
I have been out since morning.

घर पर मेरा इन्तज़ार हो रहा होगा.
Ghar par mera intezaar ho raha hoga.
घरपर मारी राह जोवाई रही हशे.
घरीं माझी वाट पाहात असतील.
They must be waiting for me at home.

घरवाले मेरी प्रतीक्षा कर रहे होंगे.
Gharwaale meri prateeksha kar rahay hongay.
घरवाळां मारी राह जोतां हशे.
घरचीं माणसें माझी वाट पाहात असतील.
The people at home must be waiting for me.

ऐसा न हो कि हम तुम्हारा इन्तज़ार ही करते रहें.
Esa na ho ki ham tumhaara intezaar hi karte rahen.
एम न थाय के अमे तमारी बाट ज जोया करीए.
आम्हांला तुमची वाट बघायला लावूं नका.
See that you don't keep us waiting.

आपका बड़ा इन्तज़ार किया.
Aap ka bada intezaar kiya.
तमारी घणी राह जोई
आपली फार वाट पाहिली.
I (we) waited long for you.

अब मैं ज्यादा इन्तज़ार नहीं कर सकता.
Ab men zyaada intezaar nahin kar sakta.
हवे हू वधारे राह नहीं जोई शकु.
आतां मी अधिक वाट पाहूं शकत नाहीं.
I can't wait any longer now.

कल जरूर आइये, भूलियेगा नहीं.

Kal zaroor aaiye, bhooliyega nahin.

काले जरूर आवजो, भूलशो नहीं.

उद्यां जरूर या, विसरू नका.

Please don't forget to come tomorrow.

जब तक मैं न आऊँ यहीं बैठे रहना.

Jab tak men na aaoon yahin bethay rahna.

ज्यां सुधी हुं आवुं नहीं त्यांसुधी अहीं ज बेसी रहेजो.

मी येईपर्यंत येथेंच थांबा.

Wait here till I come.

तुम वड़ी देर लगा रहे हो.

Tum badi dair laga rahe ho.

तुं बहु वार ळगाडे छे.

तुम्ही पुष्कळ वेळ लावीत आहात.

You are taking too long.

हम वहाँ वक्त पर नहीं पहुँच पायेंगे.

Ham wahaan waqt par nahin pahunch paayengay.

अमे त्यां समयसर नहीं पहोंचीए.

आम्ही तेथे वेळेवर पोहोचू शकणार नाही.

We won't be able to reach there in time.

हम वक्त से पहले पहुँचेंगे.

Ham waqt se pahlay pahunchengay.

अमे समय करतां बहेळा पहोंचीशु.

आम्ही थोडे आधीच पोहोचू.

We shall reach before time.

हम वहाँ ठीक वक़्त पर पहुँचे.
Ham wahan theek waqt par pahunchay.
अमे त्यां बराबर समयसर पहोंच्या.
आम्ही तेथे वेळेवर पोहचलो.
We reached exactly in time.

चलना हो तो तैयार हो जाओ.
Chalna ho to taiyyar ho jaao.
जवुं होय तो तैयार थई जाओ.
यावयाचे असेल, तर तयार व्हा.
Get ready if you want to come.

मैं ज़रा तैयार हो लूँ.
Men zara taiyyar ho loon.
हुं जरा तैयार थाउं.
मला जरा तयार होऊ द्या.
Let me get ready.

तुम बाद में आ जाना.
Tum baad men aa jaana.
तुं पछी आवजे. तमे पछी आवजो.
तुम्ही नंतर या.
You come afterwards.

वह अपने आप चला जायेगा.
Wuh apne aap chala jaayega
ते एनी मेळे ज चाल्यो जशे.
तो स्वतःच निघून जाईल.
He will go of his own accord.

तुम अजीब आदमी हो.
Tum ajeeb aadmi ho.
तमे विचित्र माणस छो.
तुम्ही विचित्र मनुष्य आहात.
You are a strange man.

मैं भी तुम्हारे साथ चलता हूँ.
Men bhi tumhaaray saath chalta hoon.
हुं पण तमारी साथे आवुं छुं.
मी पण तुमच्याबरोबर येतो.
I will also come with you.

मुझे पाँच बजे जगा देना.
Mujhe paanch baje jaga dena.
मने पांच वागे जगाडी देजो.
मला पाच वाजता जागे करा.
Wake me up at 5 o'clock.

उन्हें टेलीफ़ोन पर बुलाइए.
Unhen telephone par bulaaiye.
एमने टेलिफोन उपर बोलावो.
त्यांना टेलिफोनवर बोलवा.
Please call him on the telephone.

मुझे एक खास काम से बाहर जाना है.
Mujhe aik khass kaam se baahar jaana hai.
मारे एक खास कामने माटे बहार जवुं छे.
मला एका विशेष कामासाठी बाहेर जावयाचे आहे.
I have to go out for some special work.

अभी मेरा काम खत्म नहीं हुआ.
Abhi mera kaam khatm nahin hua.
हजी मारुं काम पूरुं नथी थयुं.
अजून माझे काम संपले नाही.
My work is not yet over.

मैं आपसे सलाह लेने आया हूँ.
Men aapse salaah lenay aaya hun.
हुं तमारी सलाह लेवा आव्यो छु.
मो आपला सल्ला घेण्यासाठी आलो आहे.
I have come to consult you.

मुझे तुमसे बातें करनी हैं.
Mujhe tumse baaten karni hain.
मारे तमारी साथे वात करवी छे.
मला आपल्याशी बोलावयाचे आहे.
I want to talk to you.

क्षमा कीजिये, मैं वक्त पर नहीं आ सका.
Kshama keejiye, men waqt par nahin aa saka.
माफ करो, हुं समयसर नहीं आवी शक्यो.
क्षमा करा, मी वेळेवर येऊ शकलो नाही.
Please excuse me, I could not come in time.

मैं गिरते-गिरते बचा.
Men girte girte bacha.
हुं पडतो पडतो बच्यो.
मी पडता पडता बाचलो.
was saved from falling.

वह आते आते रह गये.
Wuh aate aate rah gaye.
तेओ आवता आवता रही गया.
ते येनो मृणालं नी आलेच नाहीत.
He said he would come but didn't.

ईश्वर को धन्यवाद दो.
Ishwar ko dhanyawaad do.
इश्वरनो उपकार मानो.
ईश्वराला धन्यवाद द्या.
Thank God.

खुदा का शुक्र है.
Khudu ka shukra hai.
प्रभु नी कृपा.
ईश्वराची कृपा.
By God's grace.

सँभल कर चलना.
Sanbhal kar chalna.
संभाळीने चालजो.
सांभाळून चाला.
Walk cautiously.

इससे काम चल जायेगा.
Is se kaam chal jaayega.
एनाथी काम चालशे.
याने काम होईल.
This will serve the purpose.

बस, इतना बहुत है.
Bas, itna–bahut hai.
બસ, આટલું બહુ છે.
बस, एवढे पुष्कळ आहे.
This is quite enough.

इतना काफ़ी है.
Itna kaafi hai.
આટલું બસ છે.
एवढे पुरे आहे.
This is enough.

इनमें से कोई-सा चुन लो.
Inmense koi sa chun lo.
આમાંથી ગમે તે પસંદ કરી લો.
यापैकी कोणताही पसंत करा.
Choose any one of these.

यह आपके काम आएगा.
Yeh aap ke kaam aayega.
આ તમારે કામ આવશે.
हे आपल्या उपयोगी पडेल.
This will be useful to you.

क्यों तकलीफ़ करते हैं ?
Kyon takleef karte hain ?
શું કરવા તશલીફ લો છો ?
का त्रास घेता ?
Why do you trouble yourself ?

इसमें कोई तकलीफ़ नहीं.
Ismen koi takleef nahin.
आमां कोई तकलीफ नथी.
यात काही त्रास नाही.
This entails no trouble.

तुम बहुत दिनों से नज़र नहीं आये.
Tum bahut dinon se nazar nahin aaye
तमे घणा दिवससुधी देखाया नथी.
तुम्ही बऱ्याच दिवसात दिसला नाहीत.
You were not seen for long.

उन्होंने आपको याद किया है.
Unhonay aap ko yaad kiya hai.
तेओ तमने याद करे छे.
त्यानी आपली ओठवण केली आहे.
He remembers you.

वे आपको बुलाते हैं.
Way aapko bulaate hain.
तेओ तमने बोलावे छे.
ते आपल्याला बोलावत आहेत.
He is calling you.

उन्होंने आपको बुलाया है ।
Unhonay aap ko bulaaya hai.
तेमणे तमने बोलाव्या छे.
त्यानी आपल्याला बोलाबिले आहे.
He has called you.

हम नहीं जाते, तुम जाओ.
Ham nahin jaate, tum jaao.
अमे नथी आवता, तमे जाओ.
आम्ही नाही जात, तुम्ही जा.
We won't go, you go.

वहाँ कोई न कोई जरूर होगा.
Wahaan koi na koi zaroor hoga.
त्यां कोई ने कोई जरूर हशे.
तेथे कोणी ना कोणी जरूर असेल.
Somebody is sure to be there.

कुछ और कहना है ?
Kutchh aur kahna hai ?
बीजुं कंई कहेवुं छे ?
आणखी काही सांगायचे आहे का ?
Have you anything else to say ?

फिर से कहिए.
Phir se kahiye.
फरीथी कहो.
पुन्हा सांगा.
Please repeat.

और कुछ चाहिए ?
Aur kutchh chaahiye ?
बीजुं कंई जोईए ?
आणखी काही हवे आहे का ?
Anything more ?

मुझे कोई ऐतराज़ नहीं.
Mujhe koi etraaz nahin.
मारे कांई वांधो नथी.
माझी काहीं हरकत नाही.
I have no objection.

मुझे कोई शिकायत नहीं.
Mujhe koi shikaayat nahin.
मारे कांई फरियाद नथी.
माझी काही तक्रार नाही.
I have no complaint.

मेरा मेहनताना (पारिश्रमिक) दिलवाइये.
Mera mehanataana (paarrishramik) dilwaaiye.
मारु महेनताणुं पारिश्रमिक अपावो.
माझे मेहनताना (पारिश्रमिक) द्यायला लावा.
Please arrange for the payment of my wages.

मेरा फ़ैसला अटल है.
Mera feslaa atal hai.
मारो चुकादो अफर छे.
माझा निर्णय अटळ आहे.
My decision is final.

मेरी फ़िक्र न कीजिये.
Meri fikra na keejiye.
मारी चिंता न करशो.
माझी काळजी करू नये.
Don't worry about me.

मुझे कुछ नहीं पूछना.
Mujhe kutchh nahin poochna,
मारे कशुं पूछवुं नथी.
मला काही विचारावयाचे नाही.
I have nothing to ask.

मैं कुछ अर्ज़ करूँ ?
Men kutchh arz karoon ?
हुं एक विनंती करूँ ?
मी एक विनंती करू.
May I make a request.

ऐसी मूर्खता न करना.
Esi moorkhta na karna.
आवी मूर्खाई नहीं करता.
असा मूर्खपणा करू नका.
Don't be a fool like this.

मैं ऐसा बेवक़ूफ़ नहीं.
Men esa bevaqoof nahin
हुं एवो बेवकूफ नथी.
मी असा मूर्ख नाही.
I am not such a fool.

आपने मौक़ा खो दिया.
Aapne mauqa kho diya.
तमे अेक तक गुमावी.
आपण संधी गमावली न.
You lost the opportunity.

आप जब कहें तब आऊँ.
Aap jab kahen tab aaoon.
तमे ज्यारे कहो त्यारे आवुं.
आपण जेव्हा सांगाल तेव्हा येईन.
I shall come when you ask me to come.

आप जो कहें सो करूँ
Aap jo kahen so karoon.
तमे जे कहेशो ते करीश.
आपण जे सांगाल ते करीन.
I shall do what you ask me to do.

सब बन्दोबस्त कर रखना.
Sab bandobast kar rakhna.
बधो बंदोबस्त करी राखजो.
सारा बंदोबस्त करून ठेवा.
Keep everything in readiness.

हम आनन्द में हैं.
Ham anand men hain.
अमे आनन्दमां छीए.
आम्ही आनंदात आहोत.
We are happy.

तुम ग़लती पर हो.
Tum galti par ho.
तमे भूल करो छो.
तुम्ही चुकता आहा.
You are mistaken.

ऐसा नहीं है.
Esa nahin hai.
वात एम नथी.
असे नाही.
It is not so.

यह सफ़ेद झूठ है.
Yeh safed jhoot hai.
आ हरदम झूठुं छे.
हे सपशेल खोटे आहे.
This is a white lie. This is entirely false.

वह यहाँ अक्सर आते हैं.
Wuh yahaan aksar aate hain.
तेओ अहीं अवारनवार आवे छे.
ते येथे नेहमी येतात.
He comes here very often.

आप क्यों नहीं गये ?
Aap kyon nahin gaye ?
तमे केम न गया ?
आपण का गेला नाहीत ?
Why did you not go ?

काम की वजह से मेरा जाना नहीं हो सका.
Kaam ki wajeh se mera jaana nahin ho saka.
कामने लीधे माराथी जई शकायुं नहीं.
कामामुळे माझे जावे झाले नाही.
I could not go because of work.

आप उस दिन क्यों नहीं आये ?
Aap us din kyon nahin aaye ?
तमे ते दिवसे केम न आव्या ?
आपण त्या दिवशी का आला नाहीत ?
Why did you not come that day ?

एक ज़रूरी काम आ गया था.
Aik zaroori kaam aa gaya tha.
एक जरूरी काम आवो पडयुं हतुं.
एक जरूरीचे कामु आले होते.
There was an urgent work to be done.

ऐसी शरारत फिर न करना.
Esi shaararat phir na karna.
आवुं तोफान फरीथी न करशो.
असा दंगा पुन्हा करू नका.
Don't do such a mischief again.

ऐसा ही होगा.
Esa hi hoga.
एम ज थशे.
असेच होईल.
It will be so.

बुरा न मानियेगा.
Bura na maniyega.
खोटुं न लगाडता.
वाईट वाटून घेऊ नका.
Don't you take ill.

वह कल वाला गाना तो सुनाओ.

Wuh kalwala gaana to sunaao.

पेलुं कालवाळुं गायन तो संभळावो

ते कालचे गाणे तर ऐकवा

Sing the song that you sang yesterday.

आप एक गाना सुनाइये.

Aap aik gaana sunaiye.

तमे एक गायन संभळावो.

आपण एक गाणे म्हणा.

You please sing a song.

क्या आपको संगीत का शौक़ है ?

Kya aapko sangeet ka shauq hai ?

शुं तमने संगीतनो शोख छे ?

आपल्याला संगीताची आवड आहे काय ?

Are you interested in music ?

मुझे गाना सुनने का बहुत शौक़ है.

Mujhe gaana sunne ka bahut shauq hai.

मने गायन सांभळवानो घणो शोख छे.

मला गाणे ऐकण्याचा फार नाद आहे.

I am very fond of listening to music.

मुझे मारफ़त के गाने बहुत पसन्द आते हैं.

Mujhe maarfat ke gaane bahut pasand aate hain.

मने आध्यात्मिक गायनो बहु गमे छे.

मला आध्यात्मिक गाणी फार आवडतात.

I like spiritual songs very much.

आप बहुत अच्छा गाती हैं.
Aap bahut achchha gaati hain.
તમે બહુ સુંદર ગાઓ છો.
तुम्ही फार सुंदर गाता.
You sing very sweetly.

ये इस फ़न में उस्ताद हैं. ये इस कला में दक्ष हैं.
Ye is fan men ustaad hain. Ye is kala men daksh hain.
તે આ કલામાં પ્રવીણ છે.
हे या कलेमध्ये प्रवीण आहेत.
He is an expert in this art.

ये वाँसुरी बहुत अच्छी बजाते हैं.
Ye baansuri bahut achchhi bajaate hain.
તેઓ વાંસળી બહુ સરસ વગાડે છે.
हे वासरी फार सुंदर वाजवतात.
He plays the flute very well.

आज समता रेडियो पर गायेगी.
Aaj Samata radio par gayegi.
આજે સમતા રેડીયો પર ગાશે.
आज समता रेडिओवर गाईल.
Samata will sing over the radio to-day.

अपनी कोई नई रचना सुनाइये.
Apni koi nayee rachna sunaiye.
તમારી કોઈ નવી કવિતા સંભળાવો.
आपली काही नवीन रचना ऐकवा.
Please recite any of your new compositions.

आज के अखबार में आपका लेख छपा है.

Aaj ke akhbaar men aapka laikh chhapa hai.

आजना छापा मां तमारो लेख छपायो छे.

आजच्या वर्तमानपत्रात आपला लेख छापून आला आहे.

Your article has appeared in to-day's paper.

मुझे नाटक-सिनेमा देखने का शौक नहीं है.

Mujhe naatak-cinema daikhne ka shauq nahin hai.

मने नाटक सिनेमा जोवानो शोख नथी.

मला नाटक-सिनेमा बघण्याची अवाड नाही.

I am not fond of going to theatre or cinema.

मुझे कल इसकी याद दिलाना.

Mujhe kal iski yaad dilaana.

मने काले आनी याद देवडावजो.

उद्या मला याची आठवण द्या.

Remind me about it tomorrow.

मैं इस बारे में कुछ नहीं जानता.

Men is baaray men kuchh nahin jaanata.

हुं आ बाबतमां कशुं जाणतो नथी.

मला या बाबतीत काही ठाऊक नाही.

I know nothing in this connection.

मैं इस मामले पर विचार करूँगा.

Men is maamlay par vichaar karoonga.

हुं आ बाबत पर विचार करीश.

मी या बाबतीत विचार करीन.

I shall think over this matter.

मैं इस बारे में आपसे फिर बातें करूँगा.

Men is baaray men aapse phir baaten karoonga.

हुं आ बाबतमां तमारी साथे फरीथी वातो करीश.

मी याविषयी आपल्याशी पुन: बोलेन.

I shall talk to you about this later on.

इस विषय पर कोई बात नहीं हुई.

Is vishaya par koi baat nahin hui.

आ बाबत कोई वात थई नथी.

याविषयी काही बोलणे झाले नाही.

There was no talk on this topic.

मैं जरूर इस बात का ख्याल रखूँगा.

Men zaroor is baat ka khyaal rakhoonga.

हुं जरूर आ वातनो ख्याल राखीश.

मी ही गोष्ट लक्षात ठेवीन.

I shall surely keep this in mind.

आप जो कुछ कह रहे हैं मैं सब समझ रहा हूँ.

*Aap jo kutchh kah rahe hain men sab samajh
          raha hun.*

तमे जे कई कही रह्या छो ते बधुं हुं समजुं छुं.

आपण जे काही बोलता ते सर्व मला कळते.

I follow all that you say.

कोई गलती हो गई हो तो माफ़ करना.

Koi galti ho gayee ho to maaf karna.

कंई भूल थई होय तो माफ करजो.

काही चूक झाली असल्यास माफ करा.

Excuse me if there has been any mistake.

Please excuse me if I have made any mistake.

मेरा दिल गवाही नहीं देता.

Mera dil gawaahi nahin daita.

मारुं दिल शाख नथी पूरतुं.

माझे मन साक्ष देत नाही.

My conscience forbids me (to do this).

यह तुमने बड़ी होशियारी का काम किया.

Yeh tumne badi hoshiyaari ka kaam kiya.

आ तमे घणुं होशियारी काम कर्युं.

तुम्ही हे मोठ्या चतुराईचे काम केले.

It was very clever of you to have done this.

आप फ़िज़ूल अफ़सोस कर रहे हैं.

Aap fizool afsoas kar rahe hain.

तमे नकामी चिंता करो छो.

आपण व्यर्थ दुःख करता.

You are lamenting for no reason. You are
  unnecessarily worried.

अब मेरी सारी चिन्ता दूर हो गई.

Ab meri saari chinta door ho gayee.

हवे मारी बधी चिन्ता दूर थई गई.

आता माझी सारी चिन्ता दूर झाली.

Now all my anxiety is over.

उसे चेतावनी दे दी गई है.

Usay chetaawni daydee gayee hai.

एने चेतवणी आपी दीधी छे.

त्याला सावध केले आहे.

He has been warned.

मुझे यह सुन कर बड़ा रंज हुआ.
Mujhe yeh sunkar bada ranj hua
मने आ સાંભળીને ઘણું દુ:ખ થયું.
हे ऐकून मला फार दुःख झाले.
I was pained to hear this.

आप जरा-सी बात का बुरा मान गये.
Aap zara si baat ka bura maan gaye.
તમને તો નાનીસરખી વાતમાં ખોટું લાગી ગયું.
आपण लहानशा गोष्टीबद्दल वाईट वाटून घेत आहा.
You were offended over a trifle.

मैं आपका यह कहना नहीं मान सकता.
Men aapka yeh kahna nahin maan sakta.
હું તમારું આ કહેવું માની શકતો નથી.
मी आपले हे म्हणणं कबूल करूं शकत नाही.
I can't accept what you say.

इसका. क्या मतलब है ?
Iska kya matlab hai ?
આનો શો અર્થ છે ?
याचा अर्थ काय ?
What does this mean ?

आप निश्चित समय पर अवश्य आ जाइये.
Aap nishchit samay par awashya aa jaiye.
તમે નિશ્ચિત સમય પર જરૂર આવી જજો.
आपण ठरल्या वेळी अवश्य यावे.
Please come at the appointed time.

बड़ा मनोरंजक कार्यक्रम रखा गया है.
Bada manoranjak karyakram rakha gaya hai.
મોટો. મનોરંજન કાર્યક્રમ રાખવામાં આવ્યો છે.
मोठा मनोरंजक कार्यक्रम ठेवला गेला आहे.
A nice entertaining programme has been arranged

आज उनके यहाँ गाना होगा.
Aaj unke yahan gaana hoga.
આજે એમને ત્યાં સંગીતનો જલસો થશે.
आज त्यांच्याकडे गाणे होईल.
Today there will be a musical entertainment
  programme at his place.

आपसे मिलकर बड़ी खुशी हुई.
Aapse milkar badi khushi hui.
તમને મળીને ઘણો આનંદ થયો.
तुमच्या भेटीने फार आनंद झाला.
Very glad to meet you.

आपकी क्या ख़ातिर की जाय ?
Aap ki kya khatir kee jaaye ?
તમારી શી સેવા કરીએ ?
मा आपल्यासाठी काय करू शकतो ?
What shall I do for you.

हम आपकी कुछ ख़ातिरतवाज़अ न कर सके.
Ham aap ki kuchh khatir tawaazeh na kar sake.
અમે તમારો કંઈ આદરસત્કાર ન કરી શક્યા.
आम्ही आपले काही आतिथ्य करू शकलो नाही.
We could not entertain you properly.

उन्होंने हमारी बड़ी खातिर की. (उन्होंने हमारा
    बड़ा सत्कार किया.)

Unhonay hamaari badi khaatir ki.

(*Unhonay hamaara bada satkaar kiya*)

एमणे अमारो सारो सत्कार कर्यो.

त्यांनी आमचा खूप पाहुणचार केला.

They were very hospitable to us. They received
    us very well.

अब कब मुलाक़ात होगी ?

Ab kab mulaaqaat hogi ?

हवे क्यारे मुलाकात थशे ? हवे क्यारे मळशो ?

आता पुन्हा कधी भेट होईल ?

When shall we meet again ?

अब आप कब दर्शन देंगे ?

Ab aap kab darshan dengay ?

हवे तमे क्यारे मळशो ?

आता आपण कधी भेटणार (दर्शन देणार) ?

When will you come again ?

When will you see me again ?

आशा है रविवार को आपके दर्शन होंगे.

Aasha hai Raviwar ko aapke darshan hongay.

आशा छे के रविवारे तमे मळशो (दर्शन देशो).

रविवारी आपली भेट होईल अशी आशा आहे.

Hope to see you on Sunday.

आपके आने से बड़ा आनंद रहा.
Aap ke aanay say bada anand rahaa.
तमारा आगमनथी घणो आनन्द थयो.
आपल्या आगमनाने फार आनंद झाला.
Your visit gave me a great pleasure.

अब मुझे जाने की इजाज़त दीजिये.
Ab mujhe jaanay ki ijaazat deejive.
हवे मने जवानी रजा आपो.
आता मला जाण्याची परवानगी द्या.
Now please allow me to go.

5. आहार (Food)

कुछ हमें खिलाओगे या नहीं ?
Kuchh hamen khilaaogay ya nahin ?
अमनें कंई खवडावशो के नहीं ?
आम्हाला काही खायला द्याल की नाही ?
Aren't you going to give us something to eat ?

मुझे भूख लग रही है.
Mujhe bhookh lag rahi hai.
मने भूख लागी छे.
मला भूक लागली आहे.
I am feeling hungry.

चलो खाना खायें.
Chalo khaana khaayen.
चालो, जमी लईये·
चला, जेबू या.
Come, let us take our food.

आप क्या खायेंगे ?
Aap kya khaayengay ?
तमे शुं लेगो ?
आपण काय खाल ?
What vill you have ?

नाश्ता लाओ.
Nashta laao.
नास्तो लावो.
न्याहारी आणा.
Bing breakfast.

चखकर देखो.
Chakh kar dekho.
चाखी जुओ.
चाखून पाहा.
Just taste it.

मुझे भोजन के वक्त घर पहुँच जाना चाहिए.
Mujhe bhojan ke waqt ghar pahunch jana chaahiye.
जमवाना समये मारे घेर पहोंचवुं जोईए.
जेवण्याचे वेळी मला घरी पोहोचले पाहिजे.
I must reach home in time for meals.

आज आप हमारे साथ खाना खाइये.
Aaj aap hamaaray saath khaana khaiye.
आज तमे अमारी साथे जमनो.
आज आपण आमच्याबरोबर जेवा.
Please have your food with us today.

आपको मीठी चीज पसंद है या नमकीन ?
Aap ko meethi cheez pasand hai ya namkeen.
तमने गळी वस्तु भावे छे के खारी ?
आपल्याला गोड पदार्थ आवडतो की खारा ?
Do you prefer sweet or salty dish ? Which
dish do you prefer, sweet or salty ?

आम मेरा प्रिय फल है.
Aam mera priya phal hai.

मने केरी खूब भावे छे.
आंवा माझे आवडते फळ आहे.
The mango is my favourite fruit.

साग में मिरचें तेज़ है.
Saag men mirchen taiz hain.

शाकमां मरचुं वधारे छे.
भाजीत तिखट जास्त पडले आहे.
There are too many chillies in the vegetable dish.
The vegetable is too hot.

थोड़ा पानो और दीजिये.
Thoda paani aur deejiye.

हजी थोडुं वधारे पाणी आपो.
आणखी थोडेसे पाणी द्या.
Please give me a little more water.

क्या आपने खाना खा लिया ?
Kya aapne khaana kha liya ?

शुं तमे जमी लीधुं ?
आपण जेवलात काय ?
Have you had your meals ?
Have you finished eating ?

उन्होंने खाना नहीं खाया.
Unhonay khaana nahin khaaya.

तेमणे खाधुं नथी.
ते जेवले नाहीत.
He has not had his meals yet.

खाना परोस दिया गया है.
Khaana proas diya gaya hai.
भोजन पीरसाई गयुं छे.
जेवण वाढले आहे.
Food has been served.

खाना बहुत स्वादिष्ट बना है.
Khaana bahut swadisht bana hai.
रसोई खूब स्वादिष्ट बनी छे.
जेवण फार स्वादिष्ट झाले आहे.
This food is very delicious. The food is quite
  tasty.

आपने तो कुछ नहीं खाया.
Aap ne to kutchh nahin khaya.
तमे तो खास कांई खाधुं नहीं.
तुम्ही तर काहीच खाल्ले नाही.
You have eaten very tittle.

इनके लिए दूध लाओ.
In ke liye doodh laao.
एमने माटे दूध लावो.
यांच्यासाठी दूध आणा.
Please bring some milk for him (her).

दूध में शक्कर कम डालिये.
Doodh men shakkar kam daaliye.
दूधमां साकर ओछी नाखजो.
दुधात साखर कमी घाला.
Please put only a little sugar in the milk.

चमचा साफ़ नहीं है.
Chamcha saaf nahin hai.
चमचो साफ़ नथी.
चमचा स्वच्छ नाही.
The spoon is not clean.

लीजिए, शर्बत पीजिए.
Leejiye, sharbat peejiye.
लो, शर्बत पीओ.
घ्या, सरबत प्या.
Please have this sharbat (soft drink).

थोड़ा और लीजिए.
Thoda aur leejiye.
हजी थोडुं वधारे लो.
आणखी थोडे घ्या.
Have a little more.

एक प्याला गर्म चाय ले आओ.
Eik pyala garm chaai le aao.
एक प्यालो गरम चा लावो.
एक कप गरम चहा घेऊन या.
Bring a cup of hot tea.

आपकी चाय ठंडी हुई जा रही है.
Aap ki chaai thandi hui ja rahi hai.
आपनी चा ठंडी थती जाय छे.
आपला चहा थंड होतो आहे.
Your tea is getting cold.

मुझे चाय अच्छी नहीं लगती.
Mujhe chaai achchhi nahin lagati.
मने चा भावती नथी.
मला चहा आवडत नाही.
I don't like tea.

मुझे एक दावत में जाना है.
Mujhe aik daawat men jaana hai.
मारे एक समारभमां जवानुं छे.
मला एका मेजवानीला जायचे अहे.
I have to go to a party.

6. पोशाक (Dress)

यह कपड़ा बारह आने मीटर है.
Yeh kapda baarah aanay meter hai.
आ कपडुं बार आने मीटर छे.
हें कापड बारा आणे मीटर आहे.
This cloth is sold at twelve annas a meter.

तुम्हारी कमीज़ का कपड़ा बहुत अच्छा है.
Tumhaari qameez ka kapda bahut achchha hai.
तमारा पहेरणनुं कपडुं बहु सारुं छे.
तुमच्या शर्टंचे कापड फार चांगले आहे.
Your shirt-cloth is very good.

यह कपड़ा बहुत नर्म है.
Yeh kapda bahut naram hai.
आ कपडुं घणुं सुंवाळुं छे.
हे कापड फार मऊ आहे.
This cloth is very soft.

तुमने मेरे कपड़े कहाँ रख दिए ?
Tumne mere kapde kahan rakh diye ?
तमे मारां कपडां क्यां राख्यां छे ?
तुम्ही माझे कपडे कोठे ठेवलेत ?
Where have you kept my clothes ?

गीले कपड़े न पहनो.

Geelay kapde na pahno.

भीनां कपडां पहेरो नहीं.

ओले कपडे घालू नकोस.

Do not put on wet clothes.

मेरे कपड़े धोबी के घर गए हुए हैं.

Mere kapde dhobi ke ghar gaye huay hain.

मारां कपडां धोबीने घेर छे.

माझे कपडे धोब्याकडे गेलेले आहेत.

My clothes have gone to the wash.

मैं कपड़े बदल कर आता हूँ.

Men kapde badal kar aata hun.

हुं कपडां बदलीने आवुं छुं.

मी कपडे बदलून येतो.

I will come after changing my clothes.

यह साड़ी तुम्हारे वास्ते है.

Yeh saari tumhaaray waastay hai.

आ साडी तमारे माटे छे.

ही साडी तुझ्यासाठी आहे.

This sari is for you.

बच्चों को गर्म कपड़े पहना दो.

Bachchon ko garm kapde pahena do.

बाळकोंने गरम कपडां पहेरावो.

मुलांना गरम कपडे घाला.

Dress the children in woollen ones

वह केसरिया रंग की साड़ी पहने हुई थी.
Wuh kesaria rang ki saari pahenay hui thi.
तेणे केसरी रंगनी साडी पहेरी हती.
ती केशरी रंगाची साडी नेसली होती.
She had worn a saffron-coloured sari.

वह नीली वर्दी पहने हुए था.
Wuh neeli wardi pahne huay tha.
तेणे वादळी गणवेष पहेर्यो हतो.
त्याने निळा गणवेष घातला होता.
He was in a blue uniform

7. जगह (Place)

हमारा गांव सूरत जिले में है.
Hamaara gaon Surat zile men hai.
अमारुं गाम सूरत जिल्लामां छे.
आमचे गाव सुरत जिल्ह्यात आहे.
Our village is in Surat district.

मुझे यह गांव बहुत पसंद है.
Mujhe yeh gaon bahut pasand hai.
मने आ गाम घणुं पसंद छे.
मला हा गाव फार आवडतो.
I like this village very much.

यही मेरी झोंपड़ी है.
Yahi meri zhonpdi hai.
आ मारी झूंपडी छे.
हीच माझी झोपडी आहे.
This is my study room.

यह मेरा पढ़ने का कमरा है.
Yeh mera padhne ka kamra hai.
आ मारो अभ्यासनो ओरडो छे.
हीच माझी अभ्यासाची खोली आहे.
This is my study.

इस मकान का किराया क्या है ?
Is makaan ka kiraaya kya hai
आ मकाननुं भाडुं शुं छे ?
या घराचे भांडे काय आहे ?
What is the rent of this house ?

यहाँ ठंडक है.
Yahan thandak hai.
अहींयां ठंडक छे.
येथे गार आहे.
It is cool here.

वे अगले घर में रहते हैं.
Way agale ghar men rahte hain.
ते आगळना मकानमां रहे छे.
ते शेजारच्या घरात राहतात.
He lives in the adjoining house.

मैं दस वर्ष से बम्बई में रहता हूँ.
Men das varsh se Bombai men rahta hun.
हुं दस वरसथी मुंबईमां रहुं छुं.
मी दहा वर्षांपासून मुंबईत आहे.
I have been living in Bombay for the last ten
    years.

यह बड़ी खर्चीली जगह है.
Yeh badi kharcheeli jagah hai.
आ खूब खर्चाळ जग्या छे.
सी फार खर्चाची जागा आहे.
This is a very expensive place.

यहाँ बहुत मच्छर हैं.
Yahan bahut machchhar hain.
अहींयां घणा मच्छर छे.
इथे फार डांस आहेत.
This place abounds in mosquitoes.

चलो, समुद्र में नहाने चलें.
Chalo, samudra men nahane chalen.
चलो, दरिये ना'वा जईए.
चला, समुद्रात आंघोळ करायला जाऊ या.
Come on, let us go to bathe in the sea.

हम अजायबघर देखने चलेंगे.
Ham ajaayabghar dekhane chalengay.
चालो आपणे संग्रहस्थान जोवा जईए.
आपण वस्तुसग्रहालय वघायला जाऊ या.
Let us go and see the museum.

मैंने कलकत्ता नहीं देखा.
Mene Calcutta nahin dekha.
में कलकत्ता जोयुं नथी.
मी कलकत्ता पाहिले नाही.
I have not seen Calcutta.

हमारा गाँव गंगा नदी के किनारे पर है.
Hamara gaon Ganga nadi ke kinaray par hai.
अमारुं गाम गंगा नदीना कांठा पर छे.
आमचे गाव गैगा नदीच्या किनाऱ्यावर आहे.
My village is situated on the bank of the river
    Ganga.

अब वे लोग बम्बई में बस गए हैं.

Ab way loag Bombai men bas gaye hain.

હવે એ લોકો મુંબઈમાં રહે છે.

ते लोक आता मुंबईसच राहतात.

Now those people have settled down in Bombay.

8. चीज़ें (Objects)

यह बड़ी उम्दा तसवीर है.
Yeh badi umda tasweer hai.
આ ઘણી સુંદર છબી છે.
हे फार सुन्दर चित्र आहे.
This is a very fine picture.

तुमने अपना फ़ोटू नहीं दिखाया.
Tumne apna photo nahin dikhaya.
તમેં તમારો ફોટો નહીં બતાવ્યો.
तुम्ही तुमचा फोटो नाही दाखविला.
You have not shown (me) your photograph.

मुझे चश्मा बदलवाना है.
Mujhe chashma badalwana hai.
મારે ચશ્માં બદલાવવાનાં છે.
मला चष्मा बदलून घ्यायचा आहे.
I want to get my spectacles changed.

मेरी घड़ी बनने गई है.
Meri ghadi banne gayee hai.
મારી ઘડિયાળ દુરસ્ત કરાવવા આપી છે.
माझे घड्याळ दुरुस्तीला गेले आहे.
My watch has gone for repairs.
I have given my watch for repairs.

इस चाकू ने बड़ा काम दिया।
Is chaaqoo ne bada kaam diya.
आ चप्पुए भारे काम कर्यूं.
या चाकूचा चांगलाच उपयोग झाला.
The knife has given good service.

ताले में चाबी नहीं लगती।
Taale men chaabi nahin lagti.
ताळामां चावी लागती नथी.
कुलुपाला किल्ली लागत नाही
The key does not fit into the lock.

यह रस्सी मज़बूत है।
Yeh rassi mazboot hai.
आ दोरडुं मजबूत छे.
ही दोरी मजबूत आहे.
This rope is strong.

मुझसे आईना टूट गया।
Mujhse aayeena toot gaya.
माराथी अरीसो तूटी गयो.
माझ्या हातून आरसा फुटला.
The mirror was broken by me.

यह सब चीज़ें ले आओ।
Yeh sab cheezen lay aao.
आ बधी चीजो लई आवो.
या सर्व वस्तू घेऊन या.
Bring all these things.

मैंने तुम्हारी किताब नहीं देखी.

Mene tumhaari kitaab nahin dekhi.

में तमारी चोपडी (किताब) जोई नथी.

मी तुझे (तुमचे) पुस्तक पाहिले नाही.

I have not seen your book.

यह सन्दूक बहुत भारी है.

Yeh sandooq bahut bhaari hai.

आ पेटी घणी भारे छे.

ही पेटी फार जड आहे.

This box is very heavy.

यह रूमाल तुम्हारी निशानी है.

Yeh roomaal tumhari nishaani hai.

आ रूमाल तमारी निशानी छे.

हा रुमाल तुमची आठवण आहे.

The handkerchief is a mark of remembrance
    from you.

9. बाज़ार (Bazaar)

नमूना दिखाइए.
Namoona dikhaaiye.
नमूनो बतावो.
नमुना दाखवा.
Please show me a sample.

इस दरी के क्या दाम लोगे ?
Is dari ke kya daam logay?
आ शेतरंजीनी शी कीमत छे ?
या सतरंजीची किमत काय घ्याल ?
What is the price of this carpet ?

मैंने ये रूमाल तीन रुपये दर्जन खरीदे.
Mene ye roomaal teen rupaye darjan khareeday.
में आ रूमाल तण रुपये डझन खरीद्या.
मी हे रुमाल तीन रुपये डझनाप्रमाणे खरेदी केले.
I bought these handkerchiefs at three rupees a
  dozen.

यह कपड़ा किस दुकान पर मिलेगा ?
Yeh kapda kis dukaan par milega.
आ कपडं कई दुकानपर मळशे ?
हे कापड कोणत्या दुकानात मिळेल ?
At which shop is this cloth available?

अब तो दूकान बंद हो गई होगी.

Ab to dukaan band ho gayee hogi.

हवे तो दुकान बंध थई गई हशे.

आता तर दुकान बंद झाले असेल.

The shop might have been closed by now.

बाज़ार से कुछ सब्ज़ी लेते आना.

Bazaar se kuchh sabzee lete aana.

बजारमांथी शाकभाजी लई आवजो.

बाजारातून काहीतरी भाजी घेऊन या.

Bring some vegetables from the market.

मेरे साथ बाज़ार चलो.

Mere saath bazaar chalo.

मारे साथे बजारमां चालो.

माझ्याबरोबर बाजारात चला.

Come with me to the market.

क्या आप बाज़ार जा रहे हैं ?

Kya aap bazaar ja rahe hain ?

तमे बजार जाओ छो ?

आपण बाजारात चालला आहात काय ?

Are you going to the market ?

यहाँ सबसे अच्छी दुकान कौन सी है ?

Yehan sabse achchhi dukaan kaunsi hai ?

अही सौथी सारी दुकान कई छे ?

येथे सर्वात चांगले दुकान कोणते आहे ?

Which is the best shop here ?

अनाज का भाव क्या है ?
Anaaj ka bhav kya hai ?
अनाजनो भाव शुं छे ?
धान्याचा भाव काय आहे ?
What is the price of grain. ?

टमाटर कितने पैसे किलो हैं ?
Tamatar kitne paise kilo hain ?
टमेटां केटले पैसे किलो छे ?
टोमॅटो किसी पैसे किलो आहेत ?
How many paise a kilo are tomatoes ?

लौकी ताज़ी है ?
Lauki taazi hai ?
दूधी ताजी छे ?
दुध्या ताजा आहे ?
Is the gourd fresh ?

आम किस भाव बिक रहे हैं ?
Aam kis bhaav bik rahe hain ?
केरी शुं भावे वेचाय छे ?
आंबे काय भावाने विकले जात आहेत ?
What is the price of mangoes ?

आम महँगे हैं.
Aam mahengay hain.
केरी मोंघी छे.
आंबे महाग आहेत.
Mangoes are expensive.

संतरे सस्ते हैं.
Santray saste hain.
संतरां सोंघां छे.
संतरी स्वस्त आहेत.
Oranges are cheap.

केले कैसे दिये ?
Kailay kaise diye ?
केळां केम आप्यां ?
केळी कशी दिली ?
What is the price of bananas ?

वाजबी क़ीमत लेना.
Wajabi qeemat lena.
व्याजबी कींमत लेजो.
योग्य किमत घ्या.
Charge a reasonable price.

बस, बिल बना दीजिए.
Bas, bill bana deejiye.
बस, बिल बनावो.
पुरे, आता बिल बनवा.
That's all, please make the bill.

10. शारीरिक (Physical)

वह नाटा है.
Wuh naata hai.
ते ठींगणो छे.
तो ठेंगणा आहे.
He is short.

उन्हें क्या बीमारी है ?
Unhen kya beemari hai.
एमने शी बीमारी (मांदगी) छे ?
ते कशाने आजारी आहेत ?
What is he suffering from ?

कल उनकी तबियत ठीक नहीं थी.
Kal unki tabiyat theek nahin thi ?
काले तेनी तबियत सारी हती नहीं.
काल त्यांची तब्येत ठीक नव्हती.
He was not well yesterday.

वह आज कैसा है ?
Wuh aaj kesa hai ?
तेने आजे केम छे ?
आज त्याचे कसे आहे ?
How is he today ?

वह कल से आज अच्छा है.
Wuh kal se aaj achchha hai.
एने काल करतां आजे सारुं छे.
तो कालच्यापेक्षा आज बरा आहे.
He is better than (he was) yesterday.

उसके सर में दर्द है.
Uske sar men dard hai.
तेनुं माथुं दुःखे छे.
त्याचे डोके दुखत आहे.
He has a headache.

उसे जुकाम हो गया है.
Usay zukaam ho gaya hai.
तेने शरदी थइ गई छे.
त्याला सर्दी झाली आहे.
He has a cold.

वह अच्छा हो गया.
Wuh achchha ho gaya.
ते सारो थई गयो.
तो बरा झाला आहे.
He has recovered.

यह बुखार की अचूक दवा है.
Yeh bukhaar ki achook dawa hai.
तावनी आ रामबाण दवा छे.
हे तापावर रामबाण औषध आहे.
This is an infallible remedy against fever.

मैं अभी डॉक्टर को बुलाए लाता हूँ.
Men abhi doctor ko bulaye laata hoon.
हुं हमणां डॉक्टरने बोलावी लावुं छुं.
मी आत्ताच डॉक्टरला बोलावून आणतो.
I shall call the doctor just now.

तुमने दवा ली ?
Tumne dawa lee ?
तमे दवा लीधी ?
तुम्ही औषध घेतलेत ?
Did you take the medicine ?

घबराओ मत, तुम बहुत जल्द अच्छे हो जाओगे.
Ghabrao mat, tum bahut jald achchhay ho jaogay.
गभराइश नहीं, तने घणं जल्दी सारुं थई जशे.
भिऊं नका, तुम्ही अगदी लवकर बरे व्हाल.
Don't worry, you will get well soon.

तुम टहलने चलोगे न ?
Tum tahalne chalogay na ?
तमे फरवा आवशो ने ?
तुम्ही फिरायला याल ना ?
Will you come for a walk ?

मुझे नींद आ रही है.
Mujhe neend aa rahi hai.
मने ऊंघ आवे छे.
मला झोप येत आहे.
I am feeling sleepy.

दिन में नहीं सोना चाहिए.
Din men nahin sona chaahiye.
દિવસે સૂવું જોઈએ નહીં.
दिवसा निजू नये.
One should not sleep in the daytime.

आपके वहाँ बहुत सफ़ाई रहती है.
Aapke wahan bahut safaai rahti hai.
તમારે ત્યાં ઘણી ચોખ્ખાઈ રહે છે.
तुमच्याकडे फार स्वच्छता असते.
Your place is always very clean.

यह दवा दुर्बलता के लिए अक्सीर है.
Yeh dawa durbalta kay liye akseer hai.
આ દવા અશક્તિમાટે અકસીર છે.
हे औषध अशक्ततेवर रामबाण आहे.
This is an infallible remedy against debility.

11. खेल (Games)

मुन्नू खेल रहा है.
Munnu khel raha hai.
बाबो रमे छे.
ब्राबू खेळत आहे.
The baby is playing.

वह पतंग उड़ा रहा है.
Wuh patang uda raha hai.
ते पतंग उडाडे छे.
तो पतंग उडवीत आहे.
He is flying a kite.

आप कौन-से खेल खेलते हैं ?
Aap kaun se khel khailte hain ?
तमे कई रमतो रमो छो ?
आपण कोणते खेळ खेळता ?
Which games do you play ?

आओ, तुम्हें नया खेल खेलाएँ.
Aao, tumhen naya khel khelaayen.
आवो, तमने नवी रमत शीखवुं.
ब्रा, तुम्हाला नवा खेळ शिकवतों.
Come, I shall teach you a new game.

हमारी टीम जीती.
Hamaari teem jeeti.
अमारी टीम जीती.
आमचा संघ जिंकला.
Our team won.

क्या आप शतरंज खेलना चाहते हैं ?
Kya aap shatranj khelna chaahate hain ?
तमे शेतरंज रमवानुं पसंद करशो ?
आपण बुद्धिबळ खेळू इच्छिता काय ?
Do you want to play at chess ?

खेल शुरू हो गया.
Khel shuroo ho gaya.
रमत शरू थई गई.
खेळ सुरू झाला.
The game has started.

तुम्हें लाठी चलानी आती है ?
Tumhen laathi chalaani aati hai ?
तमन लाठी चलावतां आवडे छे ?
तुम्हाला लाठी फिरवायला येते काय ?
Do you know how to wield a lathi ?

12. विधिसूचक (Imperative)

मुझे कल इसकी याद दिलाना.
Mujhe kal iski yaad dilaana.
मनें काले एनी याद देवडावजो.
मला उद्या याची आठवण करा.
Remind me about this tomorrow.

पहले उन्हें बुलाकर लाओ.
Pahale unhen bula kar laao.
पहेलां तेमने बोलावी लावो.
प्रथम त्यांना बोलावून आणा.
Go and call him first.

उन्हें जगाइए नहीं, सोने दीजिए.
Unhen jagaiye nahin, sone deejiye.
तेमने जगाडो नहीं, सूवा दो.
त्यांना उठवू नका, झोपू द्या.
Do not wake him, let him sleep.

आप अपना काम कीजिए.
Aap apna kaam keejiye.
तमे तमारुं काम करो.
आपण आपले काम करा.
Please mind your own work.

बैठिए, वे अभी आते हैं.

Bethiye, way abhi aate hain.

बेसो, तेओ हुमणा आवे छे.

बसा, ते एवढ्यात येतील.

Take a seat, he is about to come.

तुम यहाँ बेफ़िक्री से रहो.

Tum yahan befikri se raho.

तमे अहीं नीरांते रहो.

तुम्ही इकडे निश्चिंत राहा.

Live here in comfort.

यहाँ शोरगुल न करो.

Yahan shoargul na karo

अहीं शोरबकोर न करो.

येथें आरडाओरडा करूं नका.

Do not make a noise here.

इतने जोर से बातें न करो.

Itne zoar se baaten na karo.

आटले मोटेथी वातो न करो.

इतक्या मोठ्याने बोलू नका.

Do not talk so loudly.

ये तश्तरियाँ अंदर ले जाओ.

Ye tashtarian ander lay' jaao.

आ रकांबीओ अंदर लई जाओ.

ह्या बश्या आंत घेऊन जा.

Take these dishes inside.

यह सब सामान हमारे घर पहुँचा दो.
Yeh sab saamaan hamaaray ghar pahuncha do.
आ बधो सामान अमारे घेर पहॉंचाडी दो.
हे सर्व सामान आमच्या घरी पोहोचवून द्या.
Send all these things to our house.

इस खत पर उसका पता लिख दीजिए.
Is khat par uska pata likh deejiye.
आ पत्रपर तेनु सरनामुं लखी आपो.
या पत्रावर त्यांचा पत्ता लिहून द्या.
Please write his address on this letter.

हमारे नाम की सब चिट्ठियाँ ले आओ.
Hamaaray naam ki sab chitthiyan lay aao.
अमारा नाम ना बधा पत्रो लई आवो.
माझ्या नावाची सर्व पत्रे घेऊन या.
Bring all the letters addressed to me.

ये सब कागजात सँभालकर रखो.
Ye sab kaagzaat sambhaal kar rakho.
आ बधा कागळो संभाळीने राखो.
हे सर्व कागद संभाळून ठेवा.
Keep all these papers carefully.

खर्चे का अंदाजा तो लगाइए.
Kharchay ka andaaza to lagaaiye.
खर्चनो अंदाज तो काढो.
खर्चाचा अदाज तर लावा.
Please calculate the expenses.

पिछली बातें भूल जाओ.
Pichhli baaten bhool jaao.
पाछली वातो भूली जाओ.
मागच्या गोष्टी विसरून जा.
Forget the past.

थोड़े दिन सब्र करो.
Thode din sabr karo.
थोडा दिवस धीरज राखो.
थोडे दिवस धीर धरा.
Have patience for a time.

किसी के नुक्स न निकालो.
Kisi ke nuqs na nikaalo.
कोईना दोष जुओ नहीं.
कोणाचेही दोष काढू नका.
Do not find fault with anybody.

कोई अच्छा सा गाना सुनाइये.
Koi achchha sa gaana sunaiye.
कोई सरस गायन संभळावो.
एखादे चांगलेसे गाणे ऐकवा.
Please sing a fine song.

13. प्रश्नबाचक (Interrogative)

ये सज्जन कौन हैं ?
Ye sajjan kaun hain ?
आ भाई कोण छे ?
हे सद्‌गृहस्थ कोण आहेत ?
Who is this gentleman ?

ये कौन साहब हैं ?
Ye kaun saaheb hain ?
आ भाई कोण छे ?
हे साहेब कोण आहेत ?
Who is this gentleman ?

वह आदमी कौन था ?
Wuh aadmi kaun tha ?
ए माणस कोण हतो ?
तो माणूस कोण होता ?
Who was that man ?

तुम क्या करते हो ?
Tum kya karte ho ?
तुमे शुं करो छो ?
तुम्ही काय करता ?
What do you do ?
What is your occupation ?

तुम्हारी उम्र क्या है ?
Tumhaari umr kya hai ?
तमारी उंमर केटली ?
तुमचे वय काय आहे ?
What is your age ?   How old are you ?

क्या वह आपको जानते हैं ?
Kya wuh aapko jaanate hain ?
शुं ते तमने ओळखे छे ?
ते आपल्याला ओळखतात काय ?
Does he know you ?

बोलो, क्या चाहते हो ?
Bolo, kya chaahate ho ?
बोलो, शुं जोईए छे ?
बोला, काय पाहिजे ?
What do you want ?

तुम कब आये ?
Tum kab aaye ?
तमे क्यारे आव्या ?
तुम्ही कधी आलात ?
When did you come ?

तुम कहाँ रहते हो ?
Tum kahaan rahte ho ?
तमे क्यां रहो छो ?
तुम्ही कोठे राहता ?
Where do you stay ?

आपका पता क्या है ?
Aapka pata kya hai ?
तमारं सरनामुं शुं छे ?
तुमचा पत्ता काय आहे ?
What is your address ?

आप क्यों चुप हैं ?
Aap kyon chup hain ?
तमे केम शांत छो ?
आपण गप्प का आहात ?
Why are you silent ?

तुम बोलते क्यों नहीं ?
Tum bolte kyon nahin ?
तमे बोलता केम नथी ?
तुम्ही बोलत का नाही ?
Why don't you speak ?

खैर तो है ?
Kher to hai ?
क्षेमकुशल तो छे ने ? बधुं हेमखेम तो छे ने ?
ठीक आहे ना ?
Is everything all right ?

क्या यह बात सच है ?
Kya yeh baat sach hai ?
शुं आ वात साची छे ?
ही गोष्ट खरी आहे काय ?
Is this a fact ?

आप क्या फ़रमाते हैं ?
Aap kya farmaate hain ?
आप शुं कहो छो ?
आपली काय आज्ञा आहे ?
What do you say, sir ?

आपको क्या पसन्द है ?
Aap ko kya pasand hai ?
तमने शुं गमे छे ?
तुम्हांला काय आवडते ?
What do you like ?

आप उनसे कब मिलेंगे ?
Aap unse kab milengay ?
तमे एमने क्यारे मळशो ?
आपण त्यांना कधी भेटाल ?
When will you see him ?
When will you meet him ?

वह आजकल कहाँ है ?
Wuh aajkal kahaan hai ?
ते आजकल क्यां छे ?
ते अलिकडे कोठे असतात ?
Where is he now-a-days ?

क्या आप एक दो दिन और नहीं ठहर सकते ?
Kya aap aik do din aur nahin thahar sakte ?
शुं तमे एक बे दिवस वधारे नहीं रोकाई शको ?
आपण आणखी एक दोन दिवस राहू शकणार नाही
    काय ?
Can you not stay for a day or two more ?

क्या आप उनका पता बता सकते हैं ?
Kya aap unka pata bata sakte hain ?
तमे एमनुं सरनामुं आपी शकशो ?
आपण त्यांचा पत्ता देऊ शकाल काय ?
Can you give me his address ?

आपको तरक्क़ी मिल गई ?
Aap ko taraqqi mil gayee ?
तमने पगारमां वधारो मळ्यो ?
आपल्याला बढती मिळाली ?
Did you get a promotion ?

उन्होंने तुम्हें कुछ दिया ?
Unhone tumhen kuchh diya ?
तेमणे तमने कईं आप्युं ?
त्यांनीं तुम्हाला काही दिले ?
Did he give you anything ?

तुम क्यों नहीं आये थे ?
Tum kyon nahin aaye thay ?
तमे केम नहोता आव्या ?
तुम्ही का आला नव्हता ?
Why did you not come ?

तुम्हें क्या हुआ था ?
Tumhen kya hua tha ?
तमने शुं थयुं हतुं ?
तुम्हाला काय झाले होते ?
What had happened to you ?
What was wrong with you ?

तुम्हें इतनी देर कहाँ लगी ?
Tumhen itani dair kahaan lagi ?
तमने आटली वार क्यां थई ?
तुम्हाला इतका वेळ कोठे लागला ?
What was it that delayed you so long ?

तुम कहाँ गये हुए थे ?
Tum kahaan gaye huay thay ?
तमे क्यां गया हता ?
तुम्ही कोठे गेला होतात ?
Where did you go ?

तुम वहाँ गये ही क्यों ?
Tum wahan gaye hi kyon ?
तमे त्यां गया ज केम ?
तुम्ही तिकडे गेलातच का ?
Why did you go there at all ?

तुम हँसते क्यों हो ?
Tum hanste kyon ho ?
तमे हसो छो केम ?
तुम्ही का हसता आहा ?
Why do you laugh ? What makes you laugh ?

अब हम क्या करें ?
Ab ham kya karen ?
हवे अमे शुं करीए ?
आता आम्ही काय करू ?
What shall we do now ?
What is to be done now ?

तुम्हें आए कितनी देर हो गई ?
Tumhen aaye kitni dair ho gayee ?
तमने आव्ये केटली वार थई ?
तुम्हाला येऊन किती वेळ झाला ?
How long is it that you are here ?

तुम यहाँ कब तक हो ?
Tum yahan kab tak ho ?
तमे अही क्यां सुधी छो ?
तुम्ही येथे किती वेळ आहात ?
How long have you been here ?

तुम्हारे लिए क्या लाऊँ ?
Tumhaaray liye kya laaon ?
तमारे माटे शुं लावुं ?
तुमच्यासाठी काय आणू ?
What shall I bring for you ?

तुम दिन भर कहाँ गायब रहे ?
Tum din bhar kahan gaayab rahe ?
तमे आखो दिवस क्यां गुम थई गया हता ?
तुम्ही दिवसभर कोठे नाहीसे झाला होतात ?
Where were you for the whole day ?

तुम कहाँ उड़ गए थे ?
Tum kahan ud gaye thay ?
तमे क्यां अदृश्य थई गया हता ?
तुम्ही कोठे नाहीसे झाला होता ?
Where did you vanish ?

बहाना क्यों बनाते हो ?
Bahaana kyon banaate ho ?
बहानुं शुं काढो छो ?
सबब का सांगतोस ?
Why are you making excuses ?

तुम सारे दिन क्या करते हो ?
Tum saaray din kya karte ho ?
तमे आखो दिवस शुं करो छे ?
तुम्ही सर्व दिवसभर काय करता ?
What do you do all day long ?

तुम मेरी खानगी बातों में क्यों दखल देते हो ?
Tum meri khangi baaton men kyon dekhal dete ho ?
तमे मारी खानगो वातोमां केम माथुं मारो छो ?
तुम्ही माइया खाजगी बाबतीत का लक्ष घालता ?
Why do you meddle in my private affairs ?

आप फ़िज़ूल क्यों ग़ुस्से होते हैं ?
Aap fizool kyon gussay hote hain ?
तमे नकामा केम गुस्से थाओ छो ?
आपण विनाकारण का रागावता ?
Why do you get angry without reason ?

यहाँ आने की तुम्हें किसने इजाज़त दी ?
Yahaan aane ki tumhen kisne ijaazat dee ?
अहीं आववानी तमने कोण रजा आपी ?
येथे येण्याची तुम्हाला कोणी परवानगी दिली ?
Who allowed you to come here ?

उन्होंने तुमसे क्या कहा ?
Unhone tumse kya kaha ?
एमणे तने शुं कह्यु ?
ते तुम्हाला काय म्हणाले ?
What did he tell you ?

क्या वहाँ जाना ज़रूरी है ?
kya wahan jaanu zaroori hai ?
शुं त्यां जवुं जरूरी छे ?
तिकडे जाणे आवश्यक (जरूर) आहे काय ?
Is it necessary to go there ?

उनका कोई खत नहीं आया ?
Unka koi khat nahin aaya ?
तेमनो कोई पत्र नथी आव्यो ?
त्यांचे काही पत्र आले नाही ?
Has there been no letter from him ?

यह सड़क कहाँ जाती है ?
Yeh sadak kahaan jaati hai ?
आ रस्तो क्यां जाय छे ?
हा रस्ता कोठे जातो ?
Where does this road lead to ?

इस कोट में कितने दाम लगे ?
Is koat men kitne daam lage ?
आ कोटनी केटली कींमत पड़ी ?
या कोटाला काय किंमत पडली ?
How much did this coat cost ?
How much did you pay for this coat ?

इसमें क्या तबदीली करूँ ?
Isemen kya tabdeeli karoon ?
आमां शुं फेरफार करुं ?
यामध्ये काय बदल करू ?
What change shall I make in it ?

इसमें क्या नुकसान है ?
Ismen kya nuqsaan hai ?
आमां शुं नुकशान छे ?
याच्यात काय नुकसान आहे ?
What harm is there ?

तुम और कहाँ-कहाँ जाओगे ?
Tum aur kahaan kahaan jaaogay ?
तमे बीजे क्यां क्यां जशो ?
तुम्ही आणखी कोठे कोठे जाल ?
Where else will you go ?

वहाँ से कब लौटोगे ?
Wahaan se kab lautogay ?
त्यांथी क्यारे पाछा आवशो ?
तेथून कधी परत याल ?
When will you return from there ?

तुम कब तक आओगे ?
Tum kab tak aaogay ?
तमे क्यांसुधीमां आवशो ?
तुम्ही केव्हा याल ?
By what time will you come ?

कितना वक्त लगेगा ?
Kitna waqt lagega ?
केटलो बखत लागशे ?
किती वेळ लागेल ?
How much time will it take ?

क्या तुमने उसका घर देखा है ?
Kya tumne uska ghar dekha hai ?
तमे एनुं घर जोयुं छे ?
तुम्ही त्याचे घर पाहिले आहे काय ?
Have you seen his house ?

क्या उसे बुलाकर लाऊँ ?
Kya usay bula kar laaon ?
शुं हुं एने बोलावी लावुं ?
त्याला बोलावून आणू काय ?
Shall I call him ?

तुम क्यों वापस चले आये ?
Tum kyon waapas chale aaye ?
तमे केम पाछा चाली आव्या ?
तुम्ही परत का आलात ?
Why did you come back ?

तुम्हारी शादी हो गई ?
Tumhaari shaadi ho gayee ?
तमारां लग्न थई गयां ?
तुमचे लग्न झाले आहे ?
Are you married ?

कुछ प्राप्ति हुई ?
Kuchh praapti hui ?
कंई मळ्यं ?
काही प्राप्ति झाली काय ?
Did you get something ?

मैं क्या कर सकता हूँ ?
Men kya kar sakta hun ?
हुं शुं करी शकुं एम छुं ?
मी काय करू शकतो ?
What can I do ?

इसके अलावा और क्या करना होगा ?
Iske alaawa aur kya karna hoga ?
आ सिवाय बीजुं शुं करवुं पडशे ?
याशिवाय आणखी काय करावे लागेल ?
What else will have to be done ?

भूलिएगा तो नहीं ?
Bhooliyega to nahin ?
भूलशो तो नहीं ने ?
विसरणार तर नाही ना ?
I hope you won't forget ?

क्या अब मैं घर जा सकता हूँ ?
Kya ab men ghar jaa sakta hun ?
हवे हुं घरे जई शकुं छुं ?
मी आता घरी जाऊ शकता काय ?
May I go home now ?

14. कुदरत (Nature)

वहाँ की आबोहवा खुश्क है.
Wahaan ki aabohawa khushk hai.
त्यांनां हवापाणी सूकां छे.
तिकडील हवा कोरडी आहे.
That place has a dry climate.

आज बड़ी गर्मी है.
Aaj badi garmi hai.
आजे घणी गरमी छे.
आज फार उकडते आहे.
It is very hot today.

बड़ी सख्त ठंड पड़ रही है.
Badi sakht thand pad rahi hai.
घणी भारे ठंडी पडी रही छे.
फार कडाक्याची थंडी पडली आहे.
It (the weather) is very cold.

बरसात शुरू हो गई.
Barsaat shuroo ho gayee.
वरसाद शरू थई गयो.
पाऊस सुरू झाला.
The rains have commenced.

बौछार आ रही है, खिड़की बंद कर दो.
Bauchhaar aa rahi hai, khidki band kar do.
वरसादनी झडी आवे छे, बारी बंध करी दो.
पावसाची झड येत आहे, खिडकी बंद करा.
The rain is beating in, close the window.

आसमान साफ हो गया.
Aasmaan saaf ho gaya.
आकाश स्वच्छ थई गयुं.
आकाश स्वच्छ झाले.
The sky is cleared.

ठंडी हवा चल रही है.
Thandi hawa chal rahi hai.
ठंडी हवा वाई रही छे.
गार वारा सुटला आहे.
A cold wind is blowing.

कैसी सुहावनी चांदनी खिल रही है !
Kesi suhaavani chaandni khil rahi hai !
केवी सुंदर चांदनी खीली रही छे !
कसे सुंदर चांदणे पडले आहे !
What a fine moonlight !

कल बड़े ज़ोर की बारिश हुई.
Kal baday zoar ki baarish hui.
काले भारे वरसाद पड्यो.
काल मुसळधार पाऊस पडला.
It rained very heavily yesterday.

ओस पड़ रही है.
Oas pad rahi hai.
झाकळ पडे छे.
दंव पडत आहे.
The dew is falling.

15. व्यक्ति (Person)

वह अच्छा आदमी है.
Wuh achchha aadmi hai.
ते सारो माणस छे.
तो चांगला माणूस आहे.
He is a good man.

वह बड़ा रहमदिल आदमी है.
Wuh bada rahamdil aadmi hai.
ते घणो दयाळु माणस छे.
तो मोठा दयाळू माणूस आहे.
He is a very kind man.

वह हज़ार में एक आदमी है.
Wuh hazaar men aik aadmi hai
ते हजारमां एक जेवो छे.
तो हजारात एक माणूस आहे.
He is one in a thousand.

यह वड़ा ज़िन्दादिल नौजवान है.
Yeh bada zindaa-dil naujawaan hai.
आ भारे खुशमिजाज नवजवान छे.
हा मोठा आनंदी तरुण आहे.
He is a very high-spirited young man.

वह बड़ी शर्मीली लड़की है.
Wuh badi sharmeeli ladki hai.
ते घणो शरमाळ छोकरी छे.
ती फार लाजाळू मुलगी आहे.
She is a very shy girl.

यह मासूम बच्ची है.
Yeh maasoom bachchi hai.
आ निर्दोष बाळकी छे.
ही निष्पाप मुलगी आहे.
She is an innocent child.

यह लड़का बड़ा होनहार है.
Yeh ladka bada honhaar hai.
आ छोकरो घणो तेजस्वी छे.
हा मुलगा फार होतकरू आहे.
He is a very promising boy.

बड़े चालाक हो जी !
Baday chaalaak ho ji !
भारे होशियार छो तमे तो !
मोठे हुशार आहात हो !
You are very clever !

तुम बड़े शरारती हो.
Tum baday sharaarati ho.
तूं घणो तोफानी छे.
तू मोठा व्रात्य आहेस.
You are very mischievous.

तुम बड़े सुस्त आदमी हो.
Tum baday sust aadmi ho.
तुं घणो आळसु माणस छे.
तू फारच आळशी माणूस आहेस.
You are a very lazy man.

वह आरामतलब है.
Wuh aaraamtalab hai.
ते आरामप्रिय छे.
तो खुशालचेंडू आहे.
He is easygoing.

वह बड़ा ज़िद्दी लड़का है.
Wuh bada ziddi ladka hai.
ते घणो जिद्दी छोकरो छे.
तो फार हट्टी मुलगा आहे.
He is a verv obstinate boy.

वह किसी की नहीं सुनता.
Wuh kisi ki nahin sunata.
ते कोईनुं सांभळतो नथी.
तो कोणाचेहि ऐकत नाही.
He listens to no one.

वह निपट गंवार है.
Wuh nipat ganwaar hai.
ते बिलकुल गमार छे.
तो अगदीच अडाणी आहे.
He is a complete simpleton. He is entirely a fool.

16. अध्ययन (Study)

वहाँ हिन्दुस्तानी की फ्री क्लासें चलती हैं.
Wahaan Hindustani ki free classen chalti hain.
त्यां हिंदुस्तानीना मफत वर्गो चाले छे.
तेथे हिंदुस्तानीचे मोफत वर्ग चालतात.
Free classes in Hindustani are held there.

आपने हिंदी की कौन-कौनसी किताबें पढ़ी हैं ?
Aapne Hindi ki kaun-kaunsi kitaben padhi hain ?
तमे हिन्दीनी कई कई चोपडीओ वांची छे ?
आपण कोणकोणती हिंदी पुस्तके वाचली आहेन ?
What books in Hindi have you read ?

तुम्हारा इम्तहान कबसे है ?
Tumhaara imtehaan kab se hai ?
तमारी परीक्षा क्यारथी छे ?
तुमची परीक्षा केव्हा आहे ?
When does your examination commence ?

कल परीक्षा है ?
Kal pareeksha hai.
काले परीक्षा छे.
उद्या परीक्षा आहे.
The examination starts tomorrow.

आज कुछ पढ़ाई नहीं हुई.
Aaj kutchh padhaayee nahin hui.
आजे कंई वंचायुं नहीं.
आज काही अभ्यास झाला नाही.
I couldn't study anything today.

इतनी जल्दी मत पढ़ो.
Itni jaldi mat padho.
आटलु उतावले वांचो नहीं.
इतक्या भरभर वाचू नकोस.
Don't read so fast.

यह सवाल आसान है.
Yeh sawaal aasaan hai.
आ सवाल सहेलो छे.
हा प्रश्न सोपा आहे.
The question is easy.

तुम ज़रूर पास होगे.
Tum zaroor pass hogay.
तमे जरूर पास थशो.
तुम्ही नक्की पास व्हाल.
You will certainly pass.

कल भूगोल का पर्चा है.
Kal bhoogoal ka parcha hai.
काले भूगोळनी परीक्षा छे.
उद्या भूगोलाचा पेपर (प्रश्नपत्र) आहे.
Tomorrow is the Geography paper.

वह गणित में कमज़ोर है.
Wuh ganit men kamzoar hai.
ते गणितमां नबळो छे.
तो गणितात कच्चा आहे.
He is weak in Mathematics.

आज वह अपना आखिरी पर्चा कर रहा है.
Aaj wuh apna aakhiri parcha kar raha hai.
आजे ते पोतानी छेल्ली परीक्षा आपी रह्यो छे.
आज तो आपला शेवटचा पेपर देत आहे.
He is doing his last paper today.

नतीजा मई के आखिर तक आएगा.
Nateeja May ke aakhir tak aayega.
परिणाम मेनी आखर सुघीमां आवी जशे.
निकाल मेच्या अखेरीला लागेल.
The result will be declared by the end of May.

इसे कुछ नहीं आता.
Ise kuchh ..ahin aata.
आने कंई आवडतुं नथी.
ह्याला काही येत नाही.
He doesn't know anything.

तुम किस स्कूल में पढ़ते हो ?
Tum kis school men padhte ho ?
तुं कई स्कूलमां भणे छे ?
तुम्ही कोणत्या शाळेत शिकता ?
In which school are you studying ?

वह पिछले सोमवार से गैरहाज़िर है.
Wuh pichhle somwaar se gerhaazir hai.
ते गया सोमवारथी गेरहाजर छे.
तो गेल्या सोमवारपासून गैरहाजर आहे.
He has been absent since Monday.

वह खूब दिल लगाकर पढ़ता है.
Wuh khoob dil laga kar padhta hai.
ते खूब दिल दईने भणे छे.
तो अगदी मन लावून अभ्यास करतो.
He takes keen interest in his studies.

मुझे हिंदी सिखाइए.
Mujhe Hindi sikhaaiye.
मने हिंदी शीखवो.
मला हिंदी शिकवा.
Please teach me Hindi.

वह परीक्षा में पास हो गया.
Wuh pareeksha men pass ho gaya.
ते परीक्षामां पास थई गयो.
तो परीक्षेत पास झाला.
He has passed the examination.

तुम्हारा स्कूल कब खुलेगा ?
Tumhaara school kab khulega ?
तमारी निशाळ क्यारे खूलशें ?
तुमची शाळा केव्हा उघडेल ?
When will your school reopen ?

तुमने आज स्कूल में क्या क्या सीखा ?
Tumne aaj school men kya-kya seekha ?
तुं आजे स्कूलमां शुं शुं शीख्यो ?
तुम्ही आज शाळेत काय काय शिकलात ?
What did you learn in school today ?

तुम किस कॉलेज में पढ़ते हो ?
Tum kis college men padhte ho ?
तमे कई कॉलेजमां भणो छो ?
तुम्ही कोणत्या कॉलेजमध्ये शिकता ?
In which college are you studying ?

तुम्हारी पढ़ाई कैसी हो रही है ?
Tumhaari padhai kesi ho rahi hai ?
तमारो अभ्यास केम चाले छे ?
तुमचा अभ्यास कसा काय चालला आहे ?
How are you getting on with your studies ?

तुम लोग इस तरह नहीं मानोगे.
Tum loag is tarah nahin maanogay.
तमे लोको आम नहीं मानो.
तुम्ही लोक ह्या तऱ्हेने नाही ऐकणार.
You people will not understand in this way.

तुम मुझे पढ़ने क्यों नहीं देते ?
Tum mujhe padhne kyon nahin daitay ?
तुं मने वांचवा केम नथी देतो ?
तुम्ही मला वाचू का देत नाही ?
Why don't you allow me to read ?

मैं आपसे कुछ कठिनाइयाँ पूछना चाहता हूँ.

Men aap se kuchh kathinaaiyan poochhna chaa hun.

हुं तमने केटलीक मुश्केलीओ पूछवा मागुं छुं.

मी आपल्याला काही शंका विचारू इच्छितो.

I want to ask about some of my difficulties.

कुछ पूछना हो तो पूछो.

Kuchh poochhna ho to poochho.

कंई पूछवु होय तो पूछो.

काही विचारावयाचे असेल तर विचारा.

If you have anything to ask, please do.

तुम्हारी पढ़ाई कहाँ तक हुई है ?

Tumhaari padhayee kahaan tak hui hai ?

तमे क्यां सुधी अभ्यास कर्यो छे ?

तुम्ही कोठपर्यंत शिकला आहात ?

How far have you studied ?

मैं आपकी बात नहीं समझा.

Men aapki baat nahin samajha.

हु तमारी वात समज्यो नहीं.

मी आपले म्हणणें समजलो नाही.

I did not understand you.

इसके क्या माने हैं ?

Iske kya maanay hain ?

आनो अर्थ शो ?

याचा अर्थ काय ?

What is the meaning of this ?

What does this mean ?

जिसको हिन्दी में क्या कहते हैं ?

Isko Hindi men kya kahate hain ?

आને હિંદીમાં શું કહેવાય ?

याला हिंदीत काय म्हणतात ?

What is this called in Hindi ?

What is the Hindi word for this ?

यह किताब मुझे अिनाम में मिली थी.

Yeh kitaab mujhe inaam men mili thi ?

आ ચોપડી મને અિનામમાં મળી હતી.

हे पुस्तक मला बक्षीस मिळाले होते.

I got this book as a prize.

17. धंधा (Profession)

आप क्या काम करते हैं ?
Aap kya kaam karte hain ?
तमे शुं धंधो करो छो ?
आपण काय काम करता ?
What is your occupation ?

वे लेखक हैं.
Way lekhak hain.
तेओ लेखक छे.
ते लेखक आहेत.
He is a writer.

आपका कारोबार ठीक चल रहा है न ?
Aap ka kaarobaar theek chal raha hai na ?
तमारु कामकाज ठीक चाली रह्युं छे ने ?
आपले कामकाज ठीक चालले आहे ना ?
Are you getting on well with your work ?

उसको नौकरी लग गई.
Usko naukari lag gayee.
तेने नोकरी मळी गई.
त्याला नोकरी लागली.
He has secured a job. He has started working.

वह नौकरी से हटा दिया गया.
Wuh naukari se hata diya gaya.
तेने नोकरीमांथी रजा मळी. तेनी नोकरी जती रही.
त्याला नोकरीवरून कमी केले.
He has been dismissed from service. He is out
of job. ·

उसे पदच्युत कर दिया गया.
Use padachyut kar diya gaya.
तेने स्थानभ्रष्ट करवामां आव्यो.
त्याला पदच्युत करण्यात आले.
He has been disgraced.

18. धन (Money)

हिसाब साफ रखो.
Hisaab saaf rakho.
हिसाब चोक्खो राखो.
हिशोब चोख ठेव.
Keep your accounts in order.

रसीद दीजिए.
Raseed deejiye.
रसीद आपो.
पावती द्या.
Please give (em) a receipt.

पैसे गिन लीजिए.
Paise gin leejiye.
पैसा गणी लो.
पैसे मोजून घ्या.
Please count the money.

यह खोटा सिक्का है.
Yeh khota sikka hai.
आ खोटो सिक्को छे.
हे खोटे नाणे आहे.
This is a counterfeit coin.

मज़दूरी ठहरा लो.
Mazdoori thera lo.
मजूरी नक्की करो.
मजुरी ठरवा.
Settle upon the wages.

वह गरीब आदमी है.
Wuh gareeb aadmi hai.
ते गरीब माणस छे
तो गरीब माणूस आहे.
He is a poor man.

तुम्हारी मज़दूरी मिल गई ?
Tumhaari mazdoori mil gayee ?
तमारी मजूरी मळी गई ?
तुमची मजुरी मिळाली ?
Did you get your wages ?

रुपया पेशगी देना होगा
Rupaya paishgi dena hoga.
बानामां रुपियो आपवो पडशे.
पैसे आगाऊ द्यावे लागतील.
Money will have to be paid in advance.

आमदनी से ज्यादा खर्च न करो.
Aamadani se zyaada kharch na karo.
आवकथी वधारे खर्च न करो.
प्राप्तीपेक्षा जास्त पैसे खर्च नका.
Don't spend more than your income.

आपके पास कितने रुपये हैं ?

Aap ke pass kitne rupaye hain ?

तमारी पासे केटला पैसा छे ?

आपल्याकडे किती पैसे आहेत ?

How much money have you ?

क्या उसने तुम्हारा वेतन दे दिया ?

Kya usne tumhaara vaitan de diya ?

शुं तेणे तमारो पगार आपी दीधो ?

त्याने तुमचा पगार दिला काय ?

Has he paid you your salary ?

इन दिनों उसे पैसे की तंगी है.

In dinon usay paise ki tangi hai

आ दिवसोमां तेने पैसानी तंगी छे

हल्ली त्याला पैशाची अडचण आहे.

He is short of money these days

वह तीन सो रुपये से कम न लेगा.

Wuh teen sau rupaye se kam na lega.

ते त्रणसो रुपियाथी औछु नहीं ले.

तो तीनशे रुपयांपेक्षा कमी घेणार नाही.

He will not accept less than three hundred rupee

वे सब खुशहाल हैं.

Way sab khushhaal hain.

तेओ बधां मजामां छे.

ते सर्व खुशाल आहेत.

They are all well.

मेरे पास नक़द रुपया नहीं है.
Mere pass naqd rupaya nahin hai.
મારી પાસે રોકડા પૈસા નથી.
माझ्याकडे रोख पैसे नाहींत.
I have no hard cash.

रुपये की क्या कमी है !
Rupaye ki kya kami hai
પૈસાની શી ખોટ છે !
पैशाची काय कमतरता आहे.
There is no shortage of money.

मैं दौलत का भूखा नहीं.
Men daulat ka bhooka nahin.
હું પૈસાનો ભૂખ્યો નથી.
मी पैशाचा लोभी नाही.
I do not hanker after wealth.
I am not after money.

दौलत से शांति नहीं मिलती.
Daulat se shanti nahin milti.
પૈસાથી શાંતિ નથી મિળતી.
पैशाने शांति मिळत नाही.
Wealth does not bring peace.

सब रुपए खर्चें हो गए.
Sab rupaye kharch ho gaye.
બધા પૈસા ખર્ચાઈ ગયા.
सर्व पैसे खर्च झाले.
All the money has been spent.

हमारा खज़ाना खाली हो गया.

Hamaara khazaana khaali ho gaya.

अमारो खजानो खाली थई गयो.

आमची तिजोरी रिकामी झाली.

Our treasury is empty.

मुझे कई बिलों का पैसा चुकाना है.

Mujhe kai bilon ka paisa chukaana hai.

मारे केटलांय बिलोना पैसा चुकाववाना छे.

मला कित्येक बिलांचे पैसे चुकते करायचे आहेत.

I have to pay several bills.

उसने इस धन्धे में लाखों रुपये कमाए.

Usne is dhandhay men lakhon rupaye kamaaye.

ते आ धन्धामां लाखो रूपिया कमायो.

त्याने ह्या धंद्यात लाखो रुपये मिळवले (कमावले).

He has earned lakhs of rupees in this business.

19. समाचार (News)

कोई अच्छी खबर सुनाइये.
Koi achchhi khabar sunaaiye.
कंई खुशखबर संभळावो.
एखादी चांगली बातमी ऐकवा.
Let's have some good news.

ऐसा क्या काम है ?
Esa kya kaam hai ?
एवुं शुं काम छे.
असे काय काम आहे ?
What sort of work is there ?

जाते ही पत्र लिखना.
Jaate hi patra likhna.
पहोंचतांनी साथे ज पत्र लखजो.
गेल्याबरोबर पत्र पाठवा.
Write immediately on your reaching (there).

कहीं भूल न जाना.
Kahin bhool na jaana.
क्यांक भूळी न जता.
पाहा हो, विसरून जाऊ नकोस.
Anyhow don't forget (about it).

फिर मिलना.
Phir milna.
फरीथी मळजो.
परत भेटा.
We will meet again.

क्या आप उनसे आज मिलेंगे ?
Kya aap unse aaj milengay ?
शुं तमे तेमने आजे मळशो ?
आपण त्यांना आज भेटाल काय ?
Will you meet him today ?

कल का 'हिन्दुस्तान' कहाँ है ?
Kal ka 'Hindustan' kahaan hai ?
कालनुं 'हिंदुस्तान' क्यां छे ?
कालचा 'हिंदुस्तान' कोठें आहे ?
Where is yesterday's 'Hindustan' ?

आज अखबार नहीं आया.
Aaj akhbaar nahin aaya.
आजे छापुं आव्युं नहीं.
आज वर्तमानपत्र आले नाही.
The newspaper has not yet come today.

उनके आ जाने पर मुझे खबर देना.
Uuke aa jaaney par mujhe khabar dena.
तेओ आवे त्यारे मने खबर आपजो.
ते आल्यावर मला कळवा.
Inform me when he comes.

आपको मेरा खत मिला था ?
Aapko mera khat mila tha ?
तमने मारो पत्र मळ्यो हतो ?
आपल्याला माझे पत्र मिळाले होते काय ?
Did you get my letter ?

डाक लेने कौन गया है ?
Dak lene kaun gaya hai ?
टपाल लेवा कोण गयुं छे ?
टपाल आणायला कोण गेला आहे ?
Who has gone to bring the post ?

आपका पत्र अभी मिला है.
Aap ka patra abhi mila hai.
तमारो पत्र हमणां ज मळ्यो.
आपले पत्र आताच मिळाले आहे.
Your letter has just been received.

मैं उन्हें चिट्ठी लिख रहा हूँ.
Men unhen chitthi likh raha hun.
हुं तेमने पत्र लखी रह्यो छुं.
मी त्यांना पत्र लिहित आहे.
I am writing a letter to him.

उन्हें मेरा प्रणाम लिख देना.
Unhen mera pranaam likh dena.
एमने मारा प्रणाम लखजो.
त्यांना माझा नमस्कार लिहा.
Give my regards to him.

तुमने उस खत का जवाब अभी तक नहीं दिया.
Tumne us khat ka jawaab abhi tak nahin diya.
तमे ते पत्रनो जवाब हजुसुधी आप्यो नथी.
तुम्ही त्या पत्राचे उत्तर अजूनपर्यंत लिहिले नाहीं.
You have not replied to that letter uptill now

बहुत दिनों से उसका कोई समाचार नहीं मिला.
Bahut dinon se uska koi samaachaar nahin mil.
घणा दिवसथी तेना कांई समाचार मळया नथी.
पुष्कळ दिवसांत त्याची काहींच समाचार कळळा नाह
There has been no news of him for a long tim

तुम उसे खत कब लिखने वाले हो ?
Tum usay khat kab likhne wale ho ?
तमे तेने पत्र क्यारे लखवाना छो ?
तू त्याला केव्हा पत्र लिहिणार आहेस ?
When will you write to him ?

अपनी राजीखुशी का तार दो.
Apni raazi-khushi ka taar do.
तमारी राजीखुशीनो तार करो.
आपल्या खुशालीची तार करा.
Wire about your health.

मुझे टेलिफोन करना है.
Mujhe telephone karna hai.
मारे टेलिफोन करवो छे.
मला टेलिफोन करायचा आहे.
I have to make a telephone call.

आज वे रेडियो पर बोलेंगे ?
Aaj way radio par bolengay.
आजे तेओ रेडियोपर बोलशे.
आज ते रेडिओवर बोलणार आहेत.
Today he is speaking over the radio.

20. सामाजिक (Social)

आज चौपाटी पर बड़ी भीड़ थी.
Aaj Chaupati par badi bheed thi.
आजे चौपाटी पर भारे भीड़ हती.
आज चौपाटीवर खूप गर्दी होती.
There was a big crowd at Chowpatty today.

उनका जुलूस निकाला गया.
Unka juloos nikaala gaya.
तेमनुं सरघस काढवामां आव्युं.
त्यांची मिरवणूक काढली होती.
He was taken out in a procession.

उनसे मेरा परिचय नहीं.
Unse mera parichay nahin.
तेमनी साथे मारे ओळखाण नथी.
माझी त्यांच्याशी ओळख नाही.
I am not acquainted with him.

आज आज़ाद मैदान में उनका भाषण होगा.
Aaj Azad Maidan me unka bhaashan hoga.
आजे आझाद मेदानमां तेमनुं भाषण थशे.
आज आझाद मैदानात त्यांचे भाषण होईल.
He is speaking at Azad Maidan today.

बे आप से मिलकर बहुत खुश होंगे.
Way aapse milker bahut khush hongay.
तेशो तमने मळीने खुब राजी थशे.
ते आपल्या भेटीने फार खूष होतील.
He will be very happy to meet you.

मैं जलसे में जा रहा हूं.
Men jalse men jaa raha hun.
हुं मेळावडामां जाउं छुं.
मी समांरमाला जातों आहे.
I am going to attend the programme.

वह कभी-कभी हमारे यहाँ आता है.
Wuh kabhi-kabhi hamaare yahan aata hai.
ते कोई-कोई वार अमारे त्यां आवे छे.
ते आमच्याकडे केव्हा केव्हां येतात.
He comes to our place occasionally.

आज हम कई महीने बाद मिल रहे हैं.
Aaj ham kai maheenay baad mil rahe hain.
आजे अमे केटलाय महिना पछी मळीए छीए.
आज आम्ही कित्येक महिन्यांनी भेटतो आहो.
Today we are meeting after several months.

आपसे इनका परिचय कराता हूं.
Aap se inka parichay karaata hun.
तमारो तेमनी साथे परिचय कराबुं छुं.
आपली त्यांच्याशी ओळख करून देतो.
I am introducing him to you.

आप मेरे मित्र मोहन हैं.

Aap mere mitra Mohan hain.

આ મારા મિત્ર મોહન છે.

हे माझे मित्र मोहन आहेत.

He is my friend Mohan.

आप हिंदी के प्रसिद्ध लेखक हैं.

Aap Hindi ke prasiddh lekhak hain.

તેઓ હિંદીના પ્રસિદ્ધ લેખક છે.

हे हिंदीचे प्रसिद्ध लेखक आहेत.

He is a well-known Hindi writer.

मैंने आपको देखा नहीं.

Mene aap ko dekha nahin.

મેં તમને જોયા નહીં.

मी आपल्याला पाहिले नाही.

I did not see you.

आपसे मिलकर बड़ी खुशी हुई.

Aapse milkar badi khushi hui.

તમને મળીને ઘણો આનંદ થયો.

आपल्या भेटीने फार आनंद झाला.

I am very much delighted to meet you.

आप बोलेंगे ?

Aap bolengay ?

તમે બોલશો ?

आपण बोलाल ?

Will you speak ?

क्या आप भी बोलनेवाले हैं ?

Kya aap bhi bolnewale hain ?

शुं तमे पण बोलवाना छो

आपणसुद्धा बोलणार आहा काय ?

Are you also speaking ?

क्या आप तैयार हैं ?

Kya aap taiyyaar hain ?

शुं तमे तैयार छो ?

आपण तयार आहा काय ?

Are you ready ?

बस आपके आने की देर थी.

Bas aapke aane ki dair thi.

मात्र आपना आववानी वार हती.

फक्त आपल्याच येण्याची वाट पाहत होतों.

We were awaiting your arrival only.

ये लोग क्यों जमा हुए हैं ?

Ye loag kyon jama huay hain ?

आ लोको केम भेगा थया छे ?

हे लोक कशाला जमा झाले आहेत ?

Why have these people assembled ?

दोनों में राज़ीनामा हो गया.

Donon men raazinaama ho gaya.

बन्ने वच्चे सुलेहनामुं थई गयुं.

दोघांमध्ये तडजोड झाली.

An agreement was brought about between them.

सभा समाप्त हो गई.
Sabha samaapt ho gayee.
सभा पूरी थई गई.
सभा समाप्त झाली.
The meeting is over.

21. क़ानून (Law)

ये सब नक़ली दस्तावेज़ हैं.
Ye sab naqli dastaavez hain.
आ बधा बनावटी दस्तावेज छे.
हे सर्व खोटे कागदपत्र आहेत.
These are all forged documents.

यह क़ानून के ख़िलाफ़ है,
Yeh qaanoon ke khilaaf hai.
आ कायदाथी विरुद्ध छे.
हे कायद्याच्या विरुद्ध आहे.
This is against the law.

तुमने ग़ैर-क़ानूनी कार्रवाई की है.
Tumne ger-qaanooni kaarrawaaee ki hai.
तमे गेरकायदे काम कर्युं छे.
तुम्ही कायद्याविरुद्ध काम केलें आहे.
You have acted illegally.

वह बिलकुल बेगुनाह (बेक़सूर) है.
Wah bilkul begunaah (beqasoor) hai.
ते बिलकुल निर्दोष छे.
तो अगदी निर्दोषी आहे.
He is quite innocent.

तुम्हें उसका जायज़ हिस्सा देना चाहिए.
Tumhen uska jaayaz hissa dena chaahiye.
तमारे तेनो योग्य हिस्सो आपवो जोईए.
तुम्ही त्याचा योग्य हिस्सा द्यायला पाहिजे.
You should give him his legitimate share.

मेरा मुकदमा पाँच मई को है.
Mera muqadama paanch Mai ko hai.
मारा केसनी तारीख पांचमी मेनी छे.
माझा खटला पाच मे-ला आहे.
My case will come up for hearing on 5th May.

आप मेरे गवाह हैं.
Aap mere gawaah hain.
तमे मारा साक्षी छो.
आपण माझे साक्षीदार आहा.
You are my witness.

आप ही इन्साफ़ करें.
Aap hi insaaf karen.
आप ज न्याय (इन्साफ) करो.
आपणच न्याय द्या.
You yourself administer justice.

उस पर खून का अपराध लगाया गया.
Us par khoon ka apraadh lagaaya gaya.
तेना पर खूननो आरोप मूकवामां आव्यो.
त्याच्यावर खुनाचा आरोप ठेवण्यात आला.
He was accused of murder.

मुक़दमे का क्या फ़ैसला हुआ ?
Muqadame ka kya fesla hua ?
केसनो शुं फेंसलो (चुकादो) आव्यो ?
खटल्याचा काय निकाल लागला ?
What was the judgment in the case ?

उसे फाँसी दे दी गई.
Usay phaansi de di gayee.
तेने फाँसी देवाई.
त्याला फाशी देण्यात आले.
He was hanged.

इन्साफ़ का यही तकाज़ा था.
Insaaf ka yahi taqaaza tha.
न्यायनी ए ज मागणी हती.
न्यायाची हीच मागणी होती.
Justice demanded it.

उसे देशनिकाला दे दिया गया.
Usay desh-nikaala de diya gaya.
तेने देशनिकाला कर्यो.
त्याला देशातून हद्दपार करण्यात आले आहे.
He has been transported.

वहाँ बदअमनी फैली हुई है.
Wahaan bad-amni pheli hui hai.
त्यां अशांति फेलाई छे.
तेथे अशांति पसरली आहे.
There is no law and order.

वहाँ फ़ौजी क़ानून लगा दिया गया.
Wahan fauji qaanoon laga diya gaya.
त्यां लइकरी कायदो चालु करी देवामां आव्यो.
तिकडे लष्करी कायदा लागू केला आहे.
Martial law has been declared there.

उसे दो दिन हवालात में रहना पड़ा.
Usay do din hawaalaat men rahna pada.
तेने बे दिवस काची जेलमां रहेवुं पड्यु.
त्याला दोन दिवस कंदेत राहावे लागले.
He had to remain in the lock-up for two days.

वह ज़मानत पर छोड़ दिया गया.
Wuh zamaanat par chhod diya gaya.
तेने जामीन पर छोडी मूक्यो.
त्याला जमिनावर सोडला आहे.
He has been released on bail.

वह फ़रार हो गया.
Wuh faraar ho gaya.
ते भागी गयो.
तो फरारी झाला.
He has absconded.

22. समय (Time)

दिन निकले चलेंगे.
Din nikle chalengay.
दिवस ऊगतां चाली नीकळशुं.
दिवस उगवताच निघू या.
We will start at daybreak.

तुम्हें देर कैसे हो गई.
Tumhen dair kese ho gayee ?
तमने मोडुं केम थयुं ?
तुम्हाला उशीर का झाला ?
How is it that you are late ?

कितने बजे हैं ?
Kitne baje hain ?
केटला वाग्या ?
किती वाजले आहेत ?
What time is it ?

क्या वक़्त है ?
Kya waqt hai ?
केटला वाग्या ?
किती वाजले ?
What's the time ?

सवा दो बजे हैं.

Sawa do baje hain.

सवा बे वाग्या छे.

सव्वादोन वाजले आहेत.

It is quarter past two.

मुझे दो बजे जगा देना

Mujhe do baje jaga dena.

भने बे वागे जगाडजो.

मला दोन वाजता उठवा (जागें करा).

Wake me at 2 o'clock.

मैं तीन बजे जाग जाता हूँ.

Men teen baje jaag jaate hun.

हुं त्रण वाग्ये जाम्पी जाउं छुं.

मी तीन वाजता जागा होतो

I get up at three.

समय पूरा हो गया.

Samay poora ho gaya.

समय पूरो थई गयो.

वेळ पुरी झाली.

The time is up.

बे सात बजे से पहले नहीं आते.

Way saat baje se pahile nahin aate.

तेओ सात वाग्या पहेलां नथी आवता.

ते सात वाजण्यापूर्वी येत नाहीत.

He does not come before seven o'clock.

मुझे डर था कि मुझे देर हो जाएगी.
Mujhe dar tha ki mujhe dair ho jaayegi.
मने डर हतो के मने मोडुं थई जशे.
मला भीति वाटत होती की मला उशीर होईल.
I had a fear I may be late.
I was afraid I may be late.

मैं बहुत सबेरे उठता हूँ.
Men bahut saweray uthta hun.
हुं सवारमां बहु वहेलों ऊठुं छुं.
मी सकाळी फार लवकर उठता.
I get up very early in the morning.

दो-तीन दिन की ही तो बात है.
Do-teen din ki hi to baat hai.
बे-त्रण दिवसनी ज वात छे.
दोन-तीन दिवसांची तर गोष्ट आहे.
It is a matter of two or three days only.

आप किस सदी में रह रहे हैं ?
Aap kis sadi men rah rahe hain ?
तमे कई सदीमां जीवी रह्या छो ?
आपण कोणत्या शतकात राहता आहा ?
In what century are you living ?

मैं वहाँ तीन हफ़्ते रहूँगा.
Men wahaan teen hafte rahoonga.
हुं त्यां त्रण अठवाडियां रहीश.
मी तिकडे तीन आठवडे राहीन.
I shall stay there for three weeks.

मुझे वहाँ वक्त पर पहुँचना है.
Mujhe wahaan waqt par pahunchna hai.
યારે ત્યાં વખતસર પહોંચવું છે.
मला तिकडें वेळेवर पोहोचायचे आहे.
I have to reach there in time.

उस वक्त आप कहाँ थे ?
Us waqt aap kahaan thay ?
તે વખતે તમે ક્યાં હતા ?
त्यावेळी आपण कोठे होता ?
Where were you then?

मेरी घड़ी बंद हो गई है.
Meri ghadi band ho gayee hai.
મારી ઘડિયાળ બંધ પડી ગઈ છે.
माझे घड्याळ बंद पडलें आहे.
My watch has stopped.

आपकी घड़ी में कितने बजे हैं ?
Aap ki ghadi men kitne baje hain.
તમારી ઘડિયાળમાં કેટલા વાગ્યા છે ?
आपल्या घड्याळात किती व.जले आहेत ?
What time is it by your watch ?

ठीक पाँच बजे हैं.
Theek paanch baje hain.
બરાબર પાંચ વાગ્યા છે.
बरोबर पांच वाजले आहेत.
It is **exactly five** o'clock.

हमें आए बीस मिनट हो गए.
Hamen aaye bees minat ho gaye.
अमने आव्याने वीश मिनिट थई गई.
आम्हाला येऊन बीस मिनिटे झाली.
Twenty minutes have passed since we came.

तुम हमेशा देर से उठते हो.
Tum hamesha dair se uthte ho.
तुं हमेशा मोडो ऊठे छे.
तू नेहमी उशीरा उठतोस.
You always get up late.

फ़िज़ूल वक्त खराब न कीजिए.
Fizool waqt kharaab na keejiye.
नकामो वखत बगाडो नहीं.
वेक फुकट (वाया) घालवू नका.
Don't waste time.

वक्त की कोई पाबन्दी नहीं है.
Waqt ki koi paabandi nahin hai.
वखतनुं कोई बंधन नथी.
वेळेचे काही बधन नाही.
There is no restrictions as regards time.
There is no time limit.

तुम कल से काम शुरू कर दो.
Tum kal se kaam shuroo kar do.
तमे कालथी काम शरू करी दो.
तुम्ही उद्यापासून काम सुरू करा.
You commence work from tomorrow.

वह दो दिन के लिए घर जाएगा।
Wuh do din ke liye ghar jaayega.
ते बे दिवसने माटे घेर जशे.
तो दोन दिवसासाठी घरी जाईल.
He will be going home for two days.

दिन छिपे जाना।
Din chhipay jaana.
दिवस आथम्ये जजो.
दिवस मावळल्यावर जा.
You may go at sunset.

सुबह मत आना।
Subah mat aana.
सवारे आवशो नहीं.
सकाळी येऊ नकोस.
Don't come in the morning.

मैं अभी जा रहा हूँ।
Men abhi jaa raha hun.
हुं हमणां जाउं छुं.
मी आत्ता जातो आहे.
I am going just now.

मुझे देर हो गई।
Mujhe dair ho gayee.
मने मोडुं थई गयुं.
मला उशीर झाला.
I was late.

उनको गये दो वर्ष हो गये.
Unko gaye do varsh ho gaye.
तेमने गये बे वर्ष थई गयां.
त्यांना अियून गेल्याला दोन वर्षे झाली.
It is two **years** since he left.

हम वहाँ देर से पहुँचे.
Ham wahaan dair se pahunchay.
अमे त्यां मोडा पहोंच्या.
आम्ही तिकडे उशिरा पोहोचलो.
We reached there late.

मैं यहाँ कल आऊँगा.
Men yahaan kal aaoonga.
हुं काले अहीं आवीश.
मी तेथे उद्या येईन.
I shall **come** here tomorrow.

23. सफर (Travel)

चलो, पैदल चलें.
Chalo, pedal chalen.
चालो, चालीने जईए.
चला, चालत जाऊ.
Come on, let us go on foot.

तेज़ चलिये.
Taiz chaliye.
जरा उतावळा चालो.
जलद (भराभर) चाला.
Please walk fast.

आपने हिन्दुस्तान के कौन-कौन से शहर देखे हैं ?
Aapne Hindustan ke kaun-kaun se shahar
  daikhay hain ?
तमे हिंस्ताननां क्यां क्यां शहेर जोयां छे ?
आपण हिंदुस्तानची कोणकोणती शहरे पाहिली आहेत ?
Which cities of India have you seen ?

यहाँ से दिल्ली कितनी दूर है ?
Yahaan se Dillee kitni door hai ?
अहींथी दिल्ही केटले दूर छे ?
येथून दिल्ली किती दूर आहे ?
How far is Delhi from here ?

लम्बा सफ़र है.
Lamba safar hai.
मुसाफरी लांबी छे.
प्रवास लांबचा आहे.
The journey is long.

वहाँ पहुँचने में कितना वक़त लगेगा ?
Wahaan pahunchne men kitna waqt lagega ?
त्यां पहोचतां केटलो वखत लागशे ?
तेथे पोहोचायला किती वेळ लागेल ?
How long will it take to reach there ?

घंटे भर का रास्ता है.
Ghantay bhar ka raasta hai.
कलाक एकनो रस्तो छे.
तासाभराचा रस्ता आहे.
It is an hour's journey.

मुझे शहर जाना है.
Mujhe shahar jaana hai.
मारे शहेरमां जवुं छे.
मला शहरात जावयाचे आहे.
I have to go to the city.

हम साथ चलेंगे.
Ham saath chalengay.
आपणे साथे जईशुं.
आपण बरोबर जाऊ या.
We shall go together.

मैं कल शाम की गाड़ी से आया था.
Men kal sham ki gaadi se aaya tha.
हुं काले सांजनी गाड़ीमां आव्यो हतो.
मी काल संध्याकाळच्या गाडीने आलो होतो.
I came by the evening train yesterday.

आप कहाँ ठहरे हुए हैं ?
Aap kahaan thaharay huay hain ?
आप क्यां ऊतर्या छो ?
आपण कोठे उतरला आहा ?
Where are you staying ?
Where have you put up ?

आपको आने में कोई दिक़्क़त तो नहीं हुई ?
Aapko aanay men koi diqqat to nahin hui ?
आपने आववामां खास तकलीफ तो नथी पडी ने ?
आपल्याला येताना त्रास तर नाही ना झाला ?
Were you put to any inconvenience while
　　coming ?

कल जुहू पर बड़ा मज़ा रहा.
Kal Juhu par bada maza raha.
काले जुहू उपर खूब मज्झा आवी.
काल जुहूला फार मजा आली.
We had a pleasant time yesterday at Juhu.

जब आप बम्बई आयें तो मुझे इत्तिला देना.
Jab aap Bombay aayen to mujhe ittila dena.
मुंबई आवो त्यारे मने खबर आपजो.
जेव्हा आपण मुंबईला याल त्या वेळी मला कळवा.
Inform me when you come to Bombay.

टिकट ले लिया ?
Ticket lay liya ?
टिकिट लई लीधी ?
तिकीट घेतले ?
Have you purchased the ticket ?

सान्ताकु्ज़ का एक वापसी टिकट दीजिये.
Santa Cruz ka aik waapasi ticket deejiye.
सान्ताक्रुजनी एक जवा-आववानी टिकिट आपो.
सान्ताक्रुजचे एक परतीचे तिकिट द्या.
Please give me a return ticket to Santa-Cruz.

वे शिमला जानेवाले हैं.
Way Simla jaanay waale hain.
तेओ सीमला जवाना छे.
ते सिमल्याला जाणार आहेत.
They will be going to Simla.

लखनऊ का कया किराया है ?
Lucknow ka kya kiraaya hai ?
लखनऊनुं शुं भाडुं छे ?
लखनौचे काय भाडे आहे ?
What is the fare to Lucknow ?

यहाँ से मद्रास के करीब पन्द्रह रुपये लगते हैं.
Yahan se Madras ke qareeb pandrah rupaye lagte hain.
अहींथी मद्रासना लागभग पंदर रूपिया थाय छे.
येथून मद्रासचे अंदाजे पंधरा रुपये होतात.
The fare to Madras from here is about fifteen rupees.

पंजाब मेल किस वक़्त छूटता है ?
Punjab Mail kis waqt chhoot-ta hai ?
पंजाब मेल केटला वागे ऊपडे छे.
पंजाब मेल किती वाजता सुटते ?
When does the Punjab Mail leave ?

मैं उन्हें लेने स्टेशन जा रहा हूँ.
Men unhen lene station jaa raha hun.
हुं एमने तेडवा स्टेशन जाउं छुं.
मी त्यांना आणायला स्टेशनवर जातो आहे.
I am going to the station to receive him.

गाड़ी किस वक़्त आती है ?
Gaadi kis waqt aati hai ?
गाडी केटला वागे आवे छे.
गाडी किती वाजता येते ?
When does the train arrive ?

गाड़ी किस प्लेटफ़ार्म पर आयेगी ?
Gaadi kis platform par aayegi ?
गाडी कया प्लॅटफॉर्म उपर आवशे ?
गाडी कोणत्या प्लॅटफॉर्मवर येईल ?
On which platform will the train arrive ?

आपका इरादा कब जाने का है ?
Aap ka iraada kab jaanay ka hai ?
तमारो विचार क्यारे जवानो छे ?
आपला कधी जाण्याचा विचार आहे ?
When do you intend going ?

मुझे दस-पच्चीस की गाड़ी पकड़नी है.
Mujhe das-pachchees ki gaadi pakadni hai.
म्हारे १०-२५ नी गाडी पकडवी छे.
मला दहापंचवीसची गाडी पकडायची आहे.
I have to catch the 10.25 train.

जल्दी कीजिए, वर्ना आपकी गाड़ी छूट जायेगी.
Jaldi keejiye, warna aapki gaadi chhoot jaayegi.
जल्दो जाव नहीं तो गाडी ऊपडी जशे.
जलदी करा नाहीतर गाडी निघून जाईल.
Make haste, or else you will miss the train.

गाड़ी छूटने वाली है.
Gaadi chhootne wali hai.
गाडी ऊपडवानी तैयारी छे.
गाडी सुटणार आहे.
The train is about to leave.

हम रास्ता भूल गये.
Ham raasta bhool gaye.
अमे रस्तो भूली गया.
आम्ही रस्ता चुकलों.
We have lost our way.

24. क्रिया (Action)

धीमे बोलिये.
Dheemay boliye.
धीमेथी बोलो.
हळू बोला.
Speak slowly.

आहिस्ता चलिये.
Aahista chaliye.
धीमेथी चालो.
सावकाश चाला.
Please walk slowly.

घर जा रहा हूँ.
Ghar jaa raha hun.
हुं घेर जाउं छुं.
घरी जातो आहे.
I'm going home.

मैं भी चलूंगा.
Men bhi chaloonga.
हुं पण आवीश.
मी सुद्धा येईन.
I will also accompany (you).
I will also join you.

मैं नहीं जाऊँगा.
Men nahin jaoonga.
हुं जईश नहीं (नहीं जाउं).
मी जाणार नाही.
I shall not go.

मैं यह नहीं कर सकता.
Men yeh nahin kar sakta.
हुं आ नहीं करी शकुं.
मी हे करू शकत नाहीं.
I cannot do this.

बहुत दिनों से मेरी मश्क छूटी हुई है.
Bahut dinon se meri mashq chhooti hui hai.
घणा दिवसोथी मने महावरो नथी.
पुष्कळ दिवसापासून माझी सवय गेलेली आहे.
For a long time I have been out of practice.

आपको क्या काम पसन्द है ?
Aap ko kya kaam pasand hai ?
आपने कयुं काम पसंद छे ?
आपल्याला कोणते काम आवडते ?
What work do you like ?

मुझे काम से फुरसत नहीं मिलती.
Mujhe kaam se fursat nahin milti.
मने कामांथी फुरसद नथी मळती.
मला कामामुळे सवड मिळत नाही.
I get no rest from work.

एक दिन में इतना काम नहीं हो सकता.

Aik din men itna kaam nahin ho sakta.

एक दिवसमां आटलुं काम न थई शके.

एका दिवसात इतके काम होणार नाही.

So much work cannot be done in a day.

मैं इस वक्त बहुत मशगूल हूँ.

Men is waqt bahut mashgool hun.

आत्यारे हुं बहु काममां छुं.

मी या वेळेला फार कामात आहे.

I am very busy at this time.

वह सख्त मेहनत करता है.

Wuh sakht mehnat karta hai.

ए सखत मेहनत करे छे.

तो पुष्कल मेहनत करतो.

He works very hard.

25. विविध (1) [Miscellaneous (1)]

साफ सुनाई नहीं देता.
Saaf sunaaee nahin deta.
बराबर संभळातुं नथी.
बरोबर ऐकू येत नाहीं.
It is not clearly audible.

कुछ सुनाई नहीं पड़ रहा.
Kuchh sunaaee nahin pad raha.
कंई संभळातं नथी.
काही ऐकू येत नव्हते.
Nothing could be heard.
Nothing was audible.

जरा जोर से बोलिये.
Zara zoar se boliye.
जरा जोरथी बोलो. जरा मोटेथी बोलो.
जरा मोठ्याने बोला.
Speak a little louder, please.

डर की कोई बात नहीं.
Dar ki koi baat nahin.
डरवानुं कोई कारण नथी.
भ्यायचे कारण नाही.
There is no cause for fear.

यहाँ कोई खतरा नहीं.
Yahaan koi khatra nahin.
अहीं कोई भय नथी
येथें काही भीति नाही.
There is no danger here.

हमें कई उज्र नहीं.
Hamen koi uzr nahin.
आमरे कांई हरकत नथी.
आमची काही हरकत नाही.
We have no objection.

मुझे कोई ऐतराज़ नहीं.
Mujhe koi etraaz nahin.
मने कई वांधो नथी.
माझी काही हरकत नाही.
I have no objection.

आप मुझ पर दबाव न डालिये.
Aap mujh par dabaav na daaliye.
तमे मारा पर दबाण न करो.
आपण माझ्यावर दडपण आणू नये.
Please don't bring pressure on me.

आप मुझे मजबूर न कीजिए.
Aap mujhe majboor na keejiye.
तमे मने लाचार न करो.
आपण मला भाग पाडू नका.
Please don't compel me.

माफ़ कीजिए, आइन्दा ऐसा नहीं होगा.
Maaf keejiye, aainda esa nahin hoga.
माफ करो, हवेथी एवुं नहीं थाय.
क्षमा करा, यापुढे असे होणार नाहीं.
Excuse me, it won't happen again.

ग़लती हुई, माफ़ कीजिए.
Galti hui, maaf keejiye.
माफ करजो, भूल थई.
चूक झाली, क्षमा करा.
Please excuse me for the mistake.

अब ऐसी भूल कभी न होगी.
Ab esi bhool kabhi na hogi.
हवे एवी भूल कदी नहीं थाय.
पुन्हा अशी चूक कधी होणार नाही.
Such a mistake will never recur.

गुस्ताख़ी माफ़.
Gustaakhi maaf.
धृष्टता माफ करो.
धाडसाबद्दल क्षमा करा.
Excuse me for my impertinence.

अपराध क्षमा कीजिए.
Apraadh kshma keejiye.
अपराध क्षमा करो.
अपराधाची क्षमा करावी (असावी).
Pardon me for my fault.

क़सूर माफ कीजिए.
Qasoor maaf keejiye.
भूल माफ करो.
चुकीची क्षमा करा.
Pardon me for my mistake.

मैं अपनी ग़लती क़बूल करता हूँ.
Men apni galti qabool kartaa hun.
हुं मारी भूल कबुल करुं छुं.
मी माझी चूक कबूल करतो.
I admit my mistake.

इस बात का सबूत क्या है ?
Is baat ka saboot kya hai ?
आ वातनो पुरावो शुं छे ?
या गोष्टीला काय पुरावा आहे ?
What is the proof for it ?

इसमें उनकी रजामन्दी है,
Ismen unki razaamandi hai.
आमां एमनी संमति छे.
याला त्यांची संमति आहे.
This has his consent.

आपकी रज़ामन्दी चाहिए.
Aap ki razaamandi chahiye.
तमारी अनुमति जोइए. •
आपली परवानगी पाहिजे.
Your consent is required.

आपको यह बात मंज़ूर है ?
Aap ko yeh baat manzoor hai ?
तमने आ बात मंज़ूर (कबूल) छे ?
आपल्याला ही गोष्ट मान्य आहे का ?
Do you accept this ?

मुझे यह शर्त मंज़ूर है.
Mujhe yeh shart manzoor hai.
मने आ शरत मंज़ूर (कबूल) छे.
मला ही अट मान्य आहे.
I accept this condition.

बस, काम बन गया.
Bas, kaam ban gaya.
बस, काम थई गयुं.
होय, काम झाले.
That's all, our task is accomplished.

अैसा न हो कि वे कहीं चल दें.
Esa na ho ki way kahin chal den.
अेवुं न थाय के तेओ क्यां कचाली जाय.
त्यानी कुठे जाऊ नये, म्हणजे झाले.
I hope he may not leave for some place or the
   other.

आज तुम बड़े खुश नज़र आते हो.
Aaj tum baday khush nazar aate ho.
आज तमे घणा खुश देखाओ छो.
आज तुम्ही खूप आनंदी दिसता.
To-day you appear to be very happy.

मैं आपकी कामयाबी पर आपको मुबारकबाद देता हूँ
Men aapki kaamyaabi par aapko mubarakbaad
  deta hun.
हुं तमारी सफलता पर तमने मुबारकबादी आपुं छुं.
मी तुमच्या यशाबद्दल तुमचे अभिनंदन करतो.
I congratulate you on your success.

यह बड़ी अजीब बात है.
Yeh badi ajeeb baat hai.
आ घणी विचित्र वात छे.
ही फार आश्चर्याची गोष्ट आहे.
It is a very strange thing.

यह बड़ी शर्म की बात है.
Yeh badi sharm ki baat hai.
आ घणी शरमनी वात छे.
ही मोठी लाजिरवाणी गोष्ट आहे.
It is a matter of great shame.

बड़े ताज्जुब की बात है.
Baday taajjub ki baat hai.
घणी आश्चर्यनी वात छे.
मोठी आश्चर्याची गोष्ट आहे.
It is a matter of great surprise.

मैं उसे ज़बान (वचन) दे चुका हूँ.
Men usay zabaan de chuka hun.
हुं तेने वचन आपी चूक्यो छुं.
मी त्याला वचन दिले आहे.
I have given him my promise.

हद हो गई !
Had ho gayee.
हद थई गई !
हद् झाली !
It has reached its climax.

तुमने सब गड़बड़ कर दिया.
Tum ne sab gadbad kar diya.
तमें बधुं बगाड़ी मार्युं.
तुम्ही घोटाळा केला.
You have spoilt the whole thing.

मुझे यकीन नहीं आता.
Mujhe yaqeen nahin aata.
मने विश्वास नथी आवतो.
मला विश्वास वाटत नाही.
I don't believe it.

मैं खुद वहाँ मौजूद था.
Men khud wahaan maujood tha.
हुं पोते त्यां हाजर हतो.
मी स्वतः तेथे हजर होतो.
I myself was present there.

मुझे इसका बड़ा कड़वा तजुर्बा है.
Mujhe iska badaa kadwa tajurba hai.
मने आनो कड़वो अनुभव थयो छे.
मला याचा फार कटु अनुभव आहे.
I have a bitter experience of this.

मामला गंभीर है.
Maamla gambheer hai.
मामलो (बाबत) गंभीर छे.
बाब गंभीर आहे.
The matter is serious.

आप भी हद करते हैं !
Aap bhi had karte hain !
तमे पण हृद करो छो !
तुम्ही पण कमाल करता !
You carry thing to extremes.

वह बहुत नियमित है.
Wuh bahut niyamit hai.
ते घणो नियमित छे.
तो फार नियमित आहे.
He is very regular.

आप दुरुस्त फ़र्माते हैं.
Aap durust farmate hain.
तमे बरोबर कहो छो.
आपण बरोबर बोलता.
What you say is right.

उनको गुस्सा आ गया.
Unko gussa aa gaya.
एमने गुस्सो चढ्यो.
त्याला राग आला.
He became angry.

मुझे तुम्हारी यह आदत पसंद नहीं.
Mujhe tumhaari yeh aadat pasand nahin.
मने तमारी आ टेव पसंद नथीं.
मला तुमची ही सवय आवडत नाही.
I don't like this habit of yours.

वे आपकी बड़ी तारीफ़ करते थे.
Way aapki badi taareef karte thay.
तेओ तमारी घणी प्रशंसा करता हता.
ते तुमची फार प्रशंसा करीत होते.
He praised you highly.

यह किताब बड़ी दिलचस्प है.
Yeh kitab badi dilchasp hai.
आ चोपडी बहु दिलचस्प छे.
हे पुस्तक फार मनोरंजक आहे.
This is a very interesting book.

आप यह किताब जरूर पढ़िये.
Aap yeh kitaab zaroor padhiye.
तमे आ पुस्तक जरूर वांचजो.
आपण हे पुस्तक जरूर वाचा.
You must read this book without fail.

रोशनी बहुत तेज है.
Roshni bahut taiz hai.
प्रकाश घणो वधारे छे.
उजेड फार जास्त आहे.
The light is very strong.

यह तो बड़ी आलीशान इमारत है.
Yeh to badi aaleshaan imaarat hai.
आ तो मोटुं आलीशान मकान छे.
ही मोठी भव्य इमारत आहे.
This is a very magnificent building.

उससे यह बेहतर है.
Us se yeh behtar hai.
पेला करतां आ वधारे सारुं छे.
ह्यापेक्षा हे जास्त चांगले आहे.
This is better than that.

यह उससे कहीं बेहतर है.
Yeh us se kahin behtar hai.
आ तेनाथी घणुं वधारे सारुं छ.
हें त्यापेक्षा पुष्कळच चांगले आहे.
This is far better than that.

यह किसी क़दर बेहतर है.
Yeh kisi qadar behtar hai.
आ कंईक वधारे सारुं छे.
हे काही अंशी अधिक चांगले आहे.
This is somewhat better.

यह तो बहुत ही अच्छा है.
Yeh to bahut hi achchha hai.
आ तो घणुं ज सारुं छे.
हे तर फार चांगले आहे.
This is superb.

यह कुछ अच्छा नहीं.
Yeh kuchh achchha nahin.
आ कंई सारुं नथी.
हे काही चांगले नाही.
This is no good,

यह किसी काम का नहीं.
Yeh kisi kaam ka nahin.
आ कंई कामनुं नथी.
हे काही कामाचे नाही.
This is quite useless.

यह बिल्कुल निकम्मी है.
Yeh bilkul nikammi hai.
आ बिल्कुल नकामी छे.
हे अगदी निरुपयोगी आहे.
This is utterly worthless.

यह फ़ैशन के खिलाफ़ है.
Yeh fashion ke khilaaf hai.
आ फैशननी विरुद्ध छे.
ते फॅशनमध्ये नाही.
This is not in fashion.

मैं आपकी राय से सहमत हूँ.
Men aapki rai se sahmat hun.
हुं तमारा मत साथे मळतो छुं.
मी तुमच्या मताचा आहें.
I concur with you in your opinion.

तुमने उसे निराश कर दिया.
Tumne usay niraash kar diya.
तमें तेने निराश कर्यो.
तुम्ही त्याला निराश केले.
You have disappointed him.

आप निराश क्यों होते हैं ?
Aap niraash kyon hote hain ?
तमे निराश केम थाव छो ?
आपण निराश का होता ?
Why do you get disappointed ?

अपने दिल से पूछो.
Apne dil se poochho.
तमारा दिलने पूछो.
आपल्या मनाला विचारा.
Ask you heart.

यह सब बेमानी है.
Yeh sab bemaani hai.
आ बधुं अर्थविनानुं छे.
हे सर्वं अर्थंहीन आहे.
All this is meaningless.

इसका कोई उपाय नहीं.
Is ka koi upai nahin.
आनो कोई उपाय नथी.
ह्याला काही उपाय नाही.
There is no remedy for this.

आपको निमंत्रण-पत्र मिला या नहीं ?

Aap ko nimantran-patra mila ya nahin ?

तमने निमंत्रण-पत्र मळ्यो के नहीं ?

आपल्याला आमंत्रणपत्र मिळाले की नाही ?

Did you get the letter of invitation or not ?

आपको शादी में ज़रूर आना पड़ेगा.

Aap ko shaadi men zaroor aana padega.

तमारे लग्नमां जरूर आववुं पडशे.

तुम्हाला लग्नाला जरूर यावे लागेल.

You will have to come to the marriage.

सारा इन्तज़ाम तुम्हारे सुपुर्द है.

Saara intzaam tumhare supurd hai.

बधी व्यवस्था तमारे माथे छे.

सर्व व्यवस्था तुमच्याकडे सोपविली आहे.

You are in charge of the whole arrangement.

मुझे अफ़सोस है कि मैं नहीं आ सकूंगा.

Mujhe afsoas hai ki men nahin aa sakoonga.

मने अफसोस छे के हुं नहीं आवी शकुं.

मी येऊ शकणार नाही याचे मला वाईट वाटते.

I regret my inability to come.

मैं इस झगड़े में नहीं पड़ना चाहता.

Men is jhagde men nahin padna chaahata.

हुं आ झगडामां पडवा नथी मागतो.

मी या भांडणात पडू इच्छीत् नाही.

I don't want to get involved in this trouble.

मैंने साफ़ इनकार कर दिया.
Mene saaf inkaar kar diya.
में चोक्खी ना कही दीधी. में स्पष्ट इनकार करी दीधो.
मी साफ नाकारले.
I refused point-blank.

यह तो मेरा फ़र्ज़ था.
Yeh to mera farz tha.
आ तो मारी फरज हती.
हे तर माझे कर्तव्य होते.
It was my duty.

तुम भी कमाल करते हो !
Tum bhi kamaal karte ho !
तमे पण कमाल करो छो !
तुम्ही अगदीं कमाल करता !
You are also taking things to the extreme.

यह आपकी ज्यादती है.
Yeh aapki zyaadati hai.
आ तमारो अत्याचार छे.
तुम्ही अतिरेक करीत आहा.
You are overdoing.

26. विविध (2) [Miscellaneous (2)]

मुझे आपसे पूरी हमदर्दी है.
Mujhe aapse poori hamdardi hai.
मने तमारा प्रत्ये पूरी सहानुभूति छे.
मला तुमच्याबद्दल पूर्ण सहानुभूति आहे.
I am entirely in sympathy with you.

मैं तुम्हारे साथ सहानुभूति प्रकट करता हूँ.
*Men tumhare saath sahaanubhooti prakat karta
  hun.*
हुं तमारा प्रत्ये सहानुभूति प्रकट करुं छुं.
मी तुमच्याबद्दल सहानुभूति प्रकट करतो.
I sympathise with you.

जो कुछ था आपके सामने पेश कर दिया.
Jo kuchh tha aapke saamne paish kar diya.
जे कंई-हतुं ते तमारी सामे मूकी दीधुं.
जे काही होते ते आपल्यापुढे सादर केले.
Whatever we had, we offered you.

तुम कैसी बहकी-बहकी बातें कर रहे हो.
Tum kesi bahki-bahki baaten kar rahe ho.
तुं केवी उडाऊ वातो करी रह्यो छे.
तू अगदीच वाह्यात गोष्टी बोलत आहेस.
What utter nonsense you are talking.

इसमें यही तो सिफ़त है.
Is men yahi to sifat hai.
आमां ए ज तो खूबी छे.
याच्यात हीच तर खुबी आहे.
This is its particular quality.

उसे रात काटना दुश्वार हो गया.
Usay raat kaatna dushwaar ho gaya.
तेने रात काढवी मुश्केल थई गई.
त्याला रात्र घालविणे कठीण झाले.
It was difficult for him to pass the night.

उन्होंने हँसकर टाल दिया.
Unhonay hans kar taal diya.
तेमणे हसीने (वात) टाळी दीधी.
त्याने ती गोष्ट हसण्यावारी नेली.
He laughed it away.

पागल हो गये हो क्या ?
Paagal ho gaye ho kya ?
गांडो थई गयो के शुं ?
वेड लागले की काय ?
Have you gone mad ?

इसमें क्या शक है ?
Is men kya shak hai ?
आमां शुं शंका छे ?
यात काय संशय ?
Is there any doubt about it ?

ये बड़ी मिन्नतों के बाद आये हैं.
Ye badi minnaton ke baad aaye hain.
तेओ घणी विनंतिओ पछी आव्या छे.
हे फार मिनतवारीने आले आहेत.
He has come after much coaxing.

हम हँसते-हँसते लोटपोट हो गये.
Ham hanste-hanste loatpoat ho gaye.
अमे हसीहसीने लोथपोथ थई गया.
हसता हसता आमची मुरकुंडी वळली.
We rocked with laughter.

वह दृश्य देखने लायक था.
Wuh drashya dekhne laayaq tha.
ते दृश्य जोवा जेवुं हतुं.
ते दृश्य पाहण्यालायक (पाहण्याजोगे) होते.
That scene was worth seeing.

यह बड़ा पेचीदा सवाल है.
Yeh bada paicheeda sawaal hai.
आ घणो अटपटो प्रश्न छे.
हा मोठा अवघड प्रश्न आहे.
This is a very intricate question.

यह तो बड़ी कठिन समस्या है.
Yeh to badi kathin samasya hai.
आ तो भारे कठण प्रश्न छे.
हा तर मोठा कठीण प्रश्न आहे.
This is a very difficult problem.

मैं शहरी ज़िन्दगी से उकता गया हूँ.
Men shahari zindgi se ukta gaya hun.
હું શહેરી જીવનથી કંટાળી ગયો છું.
मी शहरी जीवनाला कंटाळलो आहे.
I am fed up with city life.

मैंने अपनी जरूरतें बहुत कम कर दी हैं.
Mene apni zaroorten bahut kam kar di hain.
હું મારી જરૂરિયાતો ઘણી ઓછી કરી નાંખી છે.
मी माझ्या गरजा फार कमी केल्या आहेत.
I have reduced my wants to a great extent.

हमें आपकी योजना बहुत पसन्द आई.
Hamen aapki yojana bahut pasand aayee.
અમને તમારી યોજના બહુ પંસદ પડી.
आम्हाला आपली योजना फार पसंत आहे.
We liked your scheme (plan) very much.

यह तुमने बड़ी बहादुरी का काम किया.
Yeh tumne badi bahaaduri ka kaam kiya.
આ તમે ભારે બહાદુરોનું કામ કર્યું.
हे तुम्हो मोठ्या बहादुरोचे काम केले.
It was very brave on your part.

आपने बड़ी हिकमत से काम लिया.
Aap ne badi hikmat se kaam liya.
તમે ઘણી યુક્તિથી કામ લીધું.
आपण मोठ्या यूक्तीने काम केले.
You have done the work very cleverly.

मुझे उसके खिलाफ़ कोई शिकायत नहीं.
Mujhe uske khilaaf koi shikaayat nahin.
મારે એની વિરુદ્ધ કંઈ ફરિયાદ નથો.
माझी त्याच्याविरुद्ध काहीच तक्रार नाही.
I have no complaint against him.

आइन्दा तुम्हारी कोई शिकायत न आवै.
Aainda tumhaari koi shikaayat na aavay.
હવેથી તમારી કોઈ ફરિયાદ ન આવવી જોઈએ.
यापुढे तुमच्याबद्दल काही तक्रार येता कामा नये.
Let there be no complaint about you in future.

मैं कल दिन भर काम में मसरूफ़ (व्यस्त) रहा.
Men kal din bhar kaam men masroof (vyast) raha.
હું કાલે આખો દિવસભર કામમાં દટાઈ રહ્યો.
मी काल दिवसभर कामात गर्क होतों.
I war busy all day long, yesterday.

यह तो बड़ी मश्क़्क़त का काम है.
Yeh to badi mashaqqat ka kaam hai.
આ તો ઘણી મહેનતનું કામ છે.
हे तर मोठे मेहनतीचे काम आहे.
This is a very arduous task.

मैं यह बात निश्चयपूर्वक नहीं कह सकता.
Men yeh baat nishchayapoorvak nahin kah sakta.
હું આ વાત ખાતરીપૂર્વક નથી કહી શકતો.
मी ही गोष्ट नक्की सांगू शकत नाही.
I cannot say so definitely.

मुझे आपसे यही अर्ज़ करना था.
Mujhe aap se yahi arz karna tha.
મારે તમને આ જ અરજ (વિનંતિ) કરવાની હતી.
मला आपल्याकडे हीच प्रार्थना करावयाची होती.
This is all I wanted to submit to you.

यह मेरे अधिकार (अख्तियार) से बाहर है.
Yeh mere adhikaar (akhtyaar) se baahar hai.
આ મારા અધિકારની બહાર છે.
हे माझ्या अधिकाराच्या बाहेर आहे.
It is beyond my power.

मै इस मामले में कुछ नहीं कर सकता.
Men is maamlay men kuchh nahin kar sakta.
હું આ બાબતમાં કંઈ કરી શકતો નથી.
या बाबतीत मी काही करू शकत नाही.
I cannot do anything in this matter.

मैं यह ज़िम्मेवारी अपने ऊपर नहीं ले सकता.
Men yeh zimmewaari apne oopar nahin lay sakta.
હું આ જબાબદારી મારે માથે નથી લઈ શકતો.
मी ही जबाबदारी माझ्यावर घेउ शकत नाही.
I cannot take this responsibility upon myself.

तुम कैसी लचर दलीलें दे रहे हो !
Tum kesi lachar daleelen day rahe ho ¡
તમે કેવી બોદી દલીલો કરી રહ્યા છો !
तुम्ही किती लंगडा युक्तिवाद करीत आहा !
What flimsy arguments you are advancing !

आप अभी अठारहवीं सदी में ही जी रहे हैं !
Aap abhi athaarahvin sadi men hi jee rahe hain !
तमे हजी अढारमा સૈकामां ज जीवो छो !
आपण अजून अठराव्या शतकातच आहात !
You are still living in the eighteenth century !

तुम किस पसोपेश में पड़े हो ?
Tum kis pasopaish men pade ho ?
तमे शी उपाधिमां पड्या छो ?
तुम्ही कसल्या घोटाळ्यात पडला आहात ?
In what fix you are ?

मुझे इससे सैद्धान्तिक विरोध है.
Mujhe is se seddhantic virodh hai.
मारे आ साथे सिद्धांतनो वांधो छे.
माझा याला तात्विक विरोध आहे.
I am opposed to this in principle.

यह मेरे उसूल के खिलाफ़ है.
Yeh mere usool ke khilaaf hai.
आ मारा सिद्धांतथी विरुद्ध छे.
ही गोष्ट माझ्या तत्वाच्या विरुद्ध आहे.
It is against my principle.

यह मेरा सिद्धान्त है.
Yeh mera siddhant hai.
आ मारो सिद्धात छे.
हे माझे तत्व आहे.
It is my principle.

27. सभ्यता (Etiquette)

सलीका सीखो.
Saleeqa seekho.
सभ्यता शीखो.
सभ्यता शिका.
Learn some manners.

अदब से बेठो.
Adab se betho.
सभ्यतापूर्वंक बेसो.
सभ्यतापूर्वंक बसा.
Sit respectfully.

यह क्या बदतमीज़ी है !
Yeh kya bad-tameezi hai !
आ केवुं जंगलीपणुं छे !
हा काय अडाणीपणा आहे !
What rudeness !

बीच में न बोलो.
Beech men na bolo.
वच्चे न बोलो.
मध्ये बोलू नका.
Don't interrupt.

तुम बात मत काटा करो.
Tum baat mat kaata karo.
तमे वचमां न बोल्या करो.
तुम्ही बोलण्यात अडथळा आणू नका.
You should never interrupt (anyone).

शोर मचाना असभ्यता है.
Shoar machaana asabhyata hai.
घोंघाट करवो ए असभ्यता छे.
गोंगाट करणे असभ्यतेचे लक्षण आहे.
It is incivil to make noise.

बिला वजह जोर से बोलना बदतहज़बी है.
Bila wajah zoar se bolna badtahzeebi hai.
कारण वगर जोरथी बोलवुं ए असभ्यता छे.
विनाकारण जोराने बोलणे म्हणजे असभ्यता आहे.
To speak loudly without reason is bad manners.

तुम बड़े असभ्य (बदतहजीब) हो.
Tum baday asabhya (badtahzeeb) ho
तुं घणो असभ्य छे.
तू अगदीच असभ्य आहेस.
You are highly uncivilized.

वह हमारे साथ बड़ी शराफ़त से पेश आये.
Wuh hamaare saath badi sharaafat se paish aaye.
ते अमारी साथे घणी सज्जनताथी वर्त्या.
ते आमच्याशी अगदी सौजन्याने वागले.
He treated us with great courtesy.

किसी का बुरा न करो.
Kisi ka bura na karo.
कोईनुं बूरुं न करो.
कोणाचे वाईट करू नका.
Don't harm anybody.

सब का भला करो.
Sab ka bhala karo.
सौनुं भलुं करो.
सर्वांचे कल्याण करा.
Be good to all.

आम जगहों पर बीड़ी-सिगरेट नहीं पीनी चाहिए.
Aam jaghon par bidi-cigarette nahin peeni
　chaahiye.
जाहेर जग्याओमां बीड़ी-सिगरेटं पीवी जोईए नहीं.
सार्वजनिक जागी विडी-सिगरेट ओढू नये.
One should not smoke in public places.

आम जगहों पर बीड़ी-सिगरेट पीना असभ्यता है.
Aam jaghon par bidi-cigarette peena asabhyata
　hai.
जाहेर जग्याओमां बीड़ी-सिगरेट पीवी असभ्यता छे.
सार्वजनिक जागी विडी-सिगारेट ओढणे असभ्यतेंचे
　लक्षण आहे.
It is against good manners to smoke in public
　places.

पान खाकर इधर-उधर थूकते फिरना जंगलीपन की
निशानी है.

Paan khaakar idhar-udhar thookte phirna jangli-
pan ki nishaani hai.

पान खाईने ज्यां त्यां थूंकता फरवुं जंगलीपणानी
निशानी छे.

पान खाऊन जिकडे तिकडे थुंकणे जंगलीपणाचे लक्षण
आहे.

To chew betel-leaf and spit it out hither and
thither is a sign of vulgarity.

28. संभाषण (Conversation)

हमारे लिए आपको बहुत कष्ट उठाना पड़ा।
Hamaaray liye capko bahut kasht uthaana pada.
अमारे माटे तमारे घणुं कष्ट उठाववुं पड्यं.
आमच्यासाठी आपल्याला फार मेहनत घ्यावी लागली.
You had to trouble yourself a lot on account of
us.

आप क्या फ़रमा रहे थे ?
Aap kya farma rahe thay ?
तमे शुं कहेता हता ?
आपण काय म्हणत होता ?
What were you saying ?

आपने क्या इरशाद फ़रमाया ?
Aap ne kya irshaad farmaaya ?
तमे शो हुक्म फरमाव्यो ?
आपण काय हुकूम दिला ?
What did you say ?

आप क्या दर्याफ़्त फरमाते हैं ?
Aap kya daryaaft farmaate kain ?
आप शुं पूछो छो ?
आपण काय विचारीत आहा ?
What do you ask ?

आपकी महमाँनवाज़ी का शुक्रिया.
Aap ki mehmannawaazi ka shukriya.
तमारी परोणागत माटे आभार.
आपल्या पाहुणचाराबद्दल आभारी आहे.
Thanks for your hospitality.

तकल्लुफ़ न कीजिए, अपना ही घर समझिए.
Takalluf na keejiye, apna hi ghar samajhiye.
शिष्टाचार न करो, तमारुं ज घर समजो.
संकोच करू नका, आपलेच घर आहे असे समजा.
Don't stand on ceremony, make yourself at home.

इस इज़्ज़त-अफ़ज़ाई के लिए शुक्रिया.
Is izzatafzaaee kay liye shukriya.
आ मानसन्मानने माटे धन्यवाद.
या मानसन्मानाबद्दल आभार.
Thanks for this honour.

आपका पेग़ाम मुझे मिल गया था.
Aap ka pegaam mujhe mil gaya tha.
तमारो संदेशो मने मळी गयो हतो.
आपला निरोप मिळाला होता.
I got your message.

आपकी बन्दानवाज़ी का शुक्रिया
Aap ki bandanawaazi ka shukriya.
तमारी महेरबानी माटे आभार.
आपल्या मेहरबानीबद्दल आभारी आहें.
Thanks for your kindness.

आपकी ज़र्रानवाज़ी है, मैं किस लायक़ हूँ.

Aap ki zarra-nawaazi hai, men kis laayaq hun.

ए तो आपनीं मोटाई (उदारता) छे, हुं शा हिसाबमां छुं ?

हे आपले सौजन्य आहे, माझी योग्यता ती काय ?

It is your generosity, (otherwise) what am I ?

मैं आपका निहायत मशकूर हूँ. (मैं आपका अत्यंत आभारी हूँ.)

Men aapka nihaayat mashkoor hun. (Men aapka atyant aabhaari hun.)

हुं तमारो अत्यंत (घणो ज) आभारी छुं.

मी आपला अत्यंत आभारी आहें.

I am very thankful to you.

मैं आपका ऐहसानमन्द (कृतज्ञ) हूँ.

Men aapka ehsaanmand (kratagya) hun.

हुं तमारो आभारी छुं.

मी आपला आभारी (कृतज्ञ) आहें.

I am grateful to you.

मैं आपका आभारी हूँगा. (मैं आपका शुक्रगुज़ार हूँगा.)

Men aapka aabhaari hoonga. (Men aapka shukraguzaar hoonga).

हुं तमारो आभारी थईश.

मी आपला आभारी होईन.

I shall be grateful to you.

मैं आपका बड़ा शुक्रगुज़ार (आभारी) हूँ ?
Men aapka bada shukraguzaar (aabhaari) hun.
हुं तमारो घणो आभारी छुं.
मी आपला फार आभारी आहें.
I am very thankful to you.

मैं आपका तहे-दिल से शुक्रिया अदा करता हूँ.
Men aapka tahe-dil se shukriya ada karta hun.
हुं आपनो खरा अंत:करणथी आभार मानुं छुं.
मी आपले हार्दिक आभार मानतों.
I thank you from the bottom of my heart.

मैं आपको हृदय से धन्यवाद देता हूँ.
Men aapko hradaye se dhanyawaad deta hun.
हुं आपने हार्दिक धन्यवाद आपुं छुं.
मी आपणास मन:पूर्वक धन्यवाद देतो.
I thank you heartily.

मैं आपको मुबारकबाद (बधाई) देता हूँ.
Men aapko mubaarakbaad (vedhaaee) deta hun.
हुं तमने मुबारकबादी आपुं छुं.
मी आपले अभिनंदन करतों.
I congratulate you.

वधाई है !
Wadhaaee hai !
वधामणी छे !
अभिनंदन !
Congratulations !

मुलाहज़ा फ़र्माइये.
Mulahize farmaiye..
कृपा करीने आ जुओ.
कृपा करून हे पाहा.
Kindly see it.

मैं कल बहुत मशगूल था.
Men kal bahut mashgool tha.
हुं काले बहु काममां हतो.
मी काल फार कामात होतो.
I was very busy yesterday.

मुझे आपसे कुछ अर्ज़ करना है.
Mujhe aap se kuchh arz karna hai.
मारे तमने एक विनंति करवानी छे.
मला आपल्यास एक विनंती करायची आहे.
I have to make a request to you.

क्या मैं कुछ अर्ज़ कर सकता हूँ ?
Kya men kuchh arz kar sakta hun ?
शुं हुं कंई विनंती करी शकुं छुं ?
मी एक विनंती (प्रार्थना) करू शकतो काय ?
May I say something ?

यह आपका बड़ा अन्याय (बेइन्साफ़ी) है.
Yeh aap ka bada anyaay (be-insaafi) hai.
आ तमारो भारे अन्याय छे.
हा आपला भयंकर अन्याय आहे.
This is highly unjust of you.

यह बड़े अन्याय की बात है. (यह बड़ी बेइन्साफी की
   बात है).
Yeh bade anyaay ki baat hai. (Yeh badi be-
   insaafi ki baat hai.)
आ भारे गेरइन्साफनी वात छे.
ही अगदी अन्यायाची गोष्ट आहे.
This is a matter of great injustice.

यह बहुत बेजा बात है.
Yeh bahut baija baat hai.
आ घणी अनुचित वात छे.
ही फार अयोग्य गोष्ट आहे.
This is highly improper.

आपका ख्याल ग़लत है.
Aap ka khyaal galat hai.
तमारी मान्यता खोटी छे.
आपली कल्पना चुकीची आहे.
You are wrong.

इसके क्या मानी ?
Iske kya maani ?
आनों शुं अर्थ ?
याचा काय अर्थ ?
What does it mean ?

क़तअ-कलाम माफ़.
Qata-kalaam maaf.
वच्चे बोलवा माटे क्षमा.
मध्येच बोलल्याबद्दल क्षमा.
Pardon the interruption.

आप बजा फ़रमाते हैं.
Aap baja farmaate hain.

तमे ठीक कहो छो.

आपले म्हणणे बरोबर आहे.

What you say is proper.

आप दुरुस्त फ़रमाते हैं.
Aap durust farmaate hain.

तमे ठीक कहो छो.

आपण बरोबर सांगता.

What you say is right.

मैं आपकी तारीफ़ सुन चुका हूँ.
Men aapki taareef sun chuka hun.

में तमारां वखाण सांभळयां छे.

मी आपली प्रशंसा ऐकली आहे.

I have heard your praises.

कभी ग़रीबख़ाने पर भी तशरीफ़ लाइए.
(कभी हमारी कुटिया को भी पावन कीजिए.)
Kabhi gareebkhaane par bhi tashreef laaiye.
(Kabhi hamaari kutiya ko bhi paawan keejiye.)

कोईवार अमारी भूपडीने पण पावन करजो.

एकदा आमची झोपडीहि पवित्र करा.

Do come to my humble place (abode) some-
time.

आप क्या फ़रमा रहे थे ?
Aap kya farma rahe thay ?
तमे शुं कहेता हता ?
आपण काय सांगत होता ?
What were you saying ?

29. शब्द (Words)

ये रोज़मर्रा में बोले जाने वाले वाक्य हैं.
Ye roazmarra men bolay jaanay wale waakya hain.

आ रोज बोलवानां वाक्यो छे.

ही रोजच्या व्यवहारातली वाक्ये आहेत.

These sentences are used in daily speech.

चखिये तो सही.
Chakhiye to sahi.

चाखो तो खरा.

चाखून तर पहा.

Just taste.

बड़ी अच्छी खुशबू आ रही है.
Badi achchhi khushboo aa rahi hai.

घणी सरस सुगंध आवे छे.

अगदी सुरेख वास येतो आहे.

A pleasant smell is coming forth.

यह बदबू किस चीज की आ रही है ?
Yeh badboo kis cheez ki aa rahi hai ?

आ गंध कई चीजनी आवे छे ?

ही कशाची घाण येत आहे ?

From what is this foul smell issuing ?

तुम्हें खूब मश्क करनी चाहिए.
Tumhen khoob mashq karni chahiye.
तमारे खूब अभ्यास करवो जोईए.
तुम्हाला पुष्कल मेहनत केली पाहिजे.
You should practise (work) a lot.

आप यह अन्याय क्यों कर रहे हैं ?
Aap yeh anyaaya kyon kar rahe hain ?
तमे आवो अन्याय केम करो छो ?
आपण हा अन्याय का करीत आहात ?
Why are you doing this injustice ?

तुम्हारे साथ बड़ी बेइन्साफ़ी हो रही है.
Tumhaare saath badi be-insaafi ho rahi hai.
तमारा प्रत्ये भारे अन्याय थई रह्यो छे.
तुमच्या बाबतीत अगदी अन्याय होत आहे.
Gross injustice is being done to you.

वे बड़े विनोदी हैं.
Way baday vinodi hain.
तेओ खूब विनोदी छे.
ते मोठे विनोदी आहेत.
He is very jolly.

तुम बड़े बहानेबाज़ हो.
Tum baday bahaanebaaz ho.
तुं भारे बहानांखोर छे.
तुम्ही निमित्त शोघन्यान हुशार आहान.
You are clever at making excuses.

तुम बड़े नाज़ुक-मिज़ाज हो.
Tum baday naazuk-mizaaj ho.
तमे जराजरामां चिडाई जाव एवा छो.
तुम्ही अगदी हळव्या मनाचे आहात.
You are very soft-hearted.

तुम बड़े शरीर हो.
Tum baday shareer ho.
तुं घणो तोफानी छे.
तू फार वागट आहेस.
You are very mischievous.

वह बड़ा अय्याश है.
Wuh bada ayyaash hai.
ते घणो विलासी छे.
तो फार चैनी आहे.
He is a great pleasure-seeker.

यह लड़का बड़ा शरारती है.
Yeh ladka bada sharaarati hai.
आ छोकरो घणो तोफानी छे.
हा मुलगा फार सदाळ आहे.
This boy is very mischievous.

यह लड़की बड़ी नटखट है.
Yeh ladki badi natkhat hai.
आ छोकरी भारे अवळचंडी छे.
ही मुलगी फार वात्य आहे.
This girl is very naughty.

वह बड़ी खूबसूरत लड़की है.
Wuh badi khoobsoorat ladki hai.
ते घणी सुंदर छोकरी छे.
ती फार सुंदर मुलगी आहे.
She is a very beautiful girl.

वह बड़ी खुशमिजाज लड़की है.
Wuh badi khushmizaaj ladki hai.
ते घणी खुशमिजाज (आनंदी) छोकरी छे.
ती आनंदी मुलगी आहे.
She is a very jolly girl.

वह बड़ी शौकीन है.
Wuh badi shauqeen hai.
ते भारे शोखीन छे.
ती फार शोकीन आहे.
She is very fashionable.

तुम तो बहुत ही ज्यादा शर्मीली हो.
Tum to bahut hi zyaada sharmeeli ho.
तुं तो घणी ज वधारे शरमाळ छे.
तुम्ही तर फारच लाजाळू आहात.
You are exceedingly shy.

आप तो हददर्जे शर्म करती हैं.
Aap to had-darje sharm karti hain.
तमे तो वधारे पड़ती शरम राखो छो.
तुम्ही अति लाजता.
You are extremely shy.

मैंने बड़ी मुश्किल से अपना पिंड छुड़ाया.
Mene badi mushkil se apna pind chhudaaya.
में भारे मुश्केलीथी छुटकारो मेळव्यो.
मीं मोठ्या कष्टाने सुटका करून घेतली.
I disentangled myself with great difficulty.

हमें सारा प्रोग्राम मंसूख करना पड़ा.
Hamen saara program mansookh karna pada.
अमारे आखो प्रोग्राम रद करवो पड्यो.
आम्हाला सगळा कार्यक्रम रद्द करावा लागला.
We had to cancel the whole programme.

इस काम के लिए तुम जिम्मेवार हो.
Is kaam ke liye tum zimmewaar ho.
आ काम ने माटे तमे जवाबदार छो.
या कामासाठी तुम्ही जबाबदार आहात.
You are responsible for this work.

यह चीज बड़ी नुक़सानदह है.
Yeh cheez badi nuqsaandeh hai.
आ चीज घणी नुकसानकारक छे.
ही वस्तु फार नुकसानकारक आहे.
It is a very harmful thing.

यह दवा बड़ी फ़ायदेमन्द साबित हुई.
Yah dawa badi faaidemand saabit hui.
आ दवा घणी फायदाकारक साबित थई.
हे औषध खूप गुणकारी ठरले आहे.
The medicine has proved very efficacious.

उस दवा ने बड़ा नुकसान किया.
Us dawa ne bada nuqsaan kiya.

ते दवाए घणुं नुकशान कर्युं.

त्या औषधापासून पुष्कळ नुकसान झाले.

That medicine did much harm

अगर मैं बदपरहेजी न करता तो बीमार न पड़ता.
*Agar men badparhezi na karta to beemaar na
    padta.*

जो में परेजीनो भंग न क्यों होत तो बीमार न पडत.

मी कुपथ्य केले नसते पर आजारी पड़लो नसतो.

If I had not indulged in intemperance,
    I would not have fallen ill.

उसे अस्पताल में दाखिल कराना होगा
Usay aspataal men daakhil karaana hoga.

तेने इस्पितालमां दाखल कराववो पडशे.

त्याला हॉस्पिटलमध्ये दाखल करावे लागेल.

He will have to be admitted to a hospital.

उनकी हालत बहुत नाजुक है.
Unki haalat bahut naazuk hai.

तेमनी स्थिति घणी नाजुक छे.

त्यांची स्थिति अगदी नाजूक आहे.

His condition is very critical.

जरा दिमाग़ से काम लो.
Zara dimaag se kaam lo.

जरा बुद्धिपूर्वक काम करो.

जरा डोके वापरून काम करा.

Just use your brains.

इस वक़्त मेरा दिमाग़ काम नहीं दे रहा.
Is waqt mera dimaag kaam nahin de raha.
आवखते मारु मगज काम नथी करतुं.
या वेळी माझे डोके काम करीत नाही.
My brain is not working at this time.

तुम्हारे ख़िलाफ़ एक शिकायत है,
Tumhaaray khilaaf aik shikaayat hai.
तमारी सामे एक फरियाद छे.
तुमच्या विरुद्ध एक तक्रार आहे.
There is a complaint against you.

मुझे आपसे एक शिकायत है.
Mujhe aap se aik shikaayat hai.
मारे तमारी सामे एक फरियाद छे.
माझी तुमच्या बाबतीत एक तक्रार आहे.
I have a complaint against you.

आइन्दा ऐसा न करना.
Aainda esa na karna.
हवेथी एवुं नहीं करता.
यापुढे असे करू नका.
Don't do so in future.

वह मेरा जिगरी दोस्त है.
Wuh mera jigree dost hai.
ते मारो जिगरजान (दिलोजान) दोस्त छे.
तो माझा जिवलग मित्र आहे.
He is my bosom friend.

वह मेरा जानी दुश्मन है.
Wuh mera jaani dushman hai.
તે મારો જીવજાન દુશ્મન છે.
तो माझा कट्टा शत्रु आहे.
He is my deadly enemy.

आम तौर से वे सुबह घर पर ही रहते हैं.
Aam taur se way subah ghar par hi rahate hen.
સાધારણ રીતે તેઓ સવારે ઘેર રહે છે.
बहुतकरून ते सकाळी घरीच असतात.
Usually he is at home in the morning.

आज वह रोज़े से है.
Aaj wuh rozey se hai.
આજ તેને ઉપવાસ છે.
आज त्याचा उपवास आहे.
He is fasting to-day.

आज मेरा उपवास है.
Aaj mera upwaas hai.
આજે મારે ઉપવાસ છે.
आज माझा उपवास आहे.
I am fasting today.

आपको फुरसत मिल गई ?
Aap ko fursat mil gayee ?
તમને ફુરસત મળી ?
आपल्याला फुरसद मिळाली ?
So you got·some leisure after all ?

तफ़सीलवार खत लिखना.
Tafseelwar khat likhna.
विगतवार पत्र लखजो.
सविस्तर पत्र लिहा.
Write a detailed letter.

तुम खुद यह खत डालकर आओ.
Tum khud yeh khat daal kar aao.
तमे जाते ज आ पत्र नाँखीने आवो.
तुम्ही स्वतः हे पत्र टाकून या.
You go in person and post this letter.

यह तुम्हारी साजिश मालूम होती है.
Yeh tumhaari saazish maaloom hoti hai.
आ तमारु षडयंत्र मालूम पडे छे.
हे तुमचे कारस्थान आहे असें वाटतें.
This seems to be a conspiracy on your part.

तुम्हारी ये हरकतें मुझे पसन्द नहीं.
Tumhaari yeh harkaten mujhe pasand nahin.
तमारी आ रीतभात (व्यवहार) मने पसन्द नथी.
तुमचा हा व्यवहार मला आवडत नाही.
I don't like these acts of yours.

ऐसी नाजायज हरकत फिर कभी न करना.
Esi naajaayaz harkat phir kabhi na karna.
आवुं अनुचित वर्तन फरी कदी नहीं करता.
असे अयोग्य वर्तन पुन्हा कधी करूं नका.
Never behave so improperly again.

आपके होशोहृवास तो दुरुस्त हैं.
Aap ke hoshohawaas to durust hain ?
तमारा होशकोश तो ठेकाणे छे ने ?
तुम्ही शुद्धीवर आहात ना ?
Are you in your senses ?

होश की बातें करो.
Hoash ki baaten karo.
समजदारीनी वात करो.
विचार करून बोला.
Talk sense.

मामले की तहक़ीक़ात हो रही है.
Maamlay ki tehqeeqaat ho rahi hai.
मामलानी तपास थई रही छे.
प्रकरणाचा तपास चालू आहे.
The matter is under investigation.

यह सुनकर उनके होश उड़ गये.
Yeh sunkar unke hosh ud gaye.
आ सांभळीने एना होश कोश ऊडी गया.
हे ऐकून त्याचे भान हरपले.
He was stunned to hear this.

उसने साफ़ जवाब दे दिया.
Usnay saaf jawaab day diya.
तेणे चोक्खो (स्पष्ट) जवाब दई दीधो.
त्याने स्पष्ट नकार दिला.
He flatly refused.

उसने नौकरी से इस्तीफ़ा (त्यागपत्र) दे दिया.
Usnay naukari se isteefa (tyaagpatra) day diya.
तेणे नोकरीमांथी राजीनामुं आपी दीधुं.
त्याने नौकरीचा राजिनामा दिला.
He resigned his post.

आइन्दा ऐसी ग़फ़लत न होगी.
Aainda esi gaflat na hogi.
हवेथी आवी भूल नहीं थाय.
यापुढे अशी चूक होणार नाही.
There will be no such mistake in future.

आपकी मन्तक़ ही निराली है.
Aap ki mantaq hi niraali hai.
तमारुं तर्कशास्त्र ज अनोखुं छे.
आपले तर्कशास्त्रच चमत्कारीक आहे.
Your logic is queer.

आपकी युक्ति तर्कसम्मत नहीं.
Aap ki yukti tarksammat nahin.
तमारी दलील तर्कयुक्त नथी.
आपली युक्ति तर्काला धरून (तर्कशुद्ध) नाही.
आपला मुद्दा तर्कशुद्ध नाही.
Your argument is not logical.

गांधीजी बड़े हरदिलअज़ीज़ (लोकप्रिय) थे.
Gandhiji baday hardilazeez (loakpriya) thay.
गांधीजी घणा लोकप्रिय हता.
गांधीजी फार लोकप्रिय होते.
Gandhiji was very popular.

30. उच्च (Higher)

क्या ख़ुशनुमा नज़्ज़ारा है !
(कैसा मनोहर दृश्य है !)
Kya khushnuma nazzaara hai !
केवुं सुंदर दृश्य छे !
किती मनोहर दृश्य आहे !
What a fine scenery !

कैसा सुंदर दृश्य है !
Kesa sundar drashya hai !
केत्रो सुंदर देखाव छे !
कसा सुंदर देखावा आहे !
What a beautiful scene !

सद्गुण सबसे अच्छे ज़ेवर हैं.
Sadgun sab se achchhe zaiwar hain.
सद्गुण सौथी सरस घरेणुं छे.
सद्गुण सर्वात चांगले आभूषण आहे.
Virtues are the best ornaments.

आपके ख्यालात बहुत ऊँचे हैं.
Aap ke khyaalaat bahut oonchay hain.
तमारा विचारो घणा ऊँचा छे.
तुमचे विचार फार उच्च आहेत.
You thoughts are very high.

तुम तो शायरी करने लगे !
Tum to shayari karne lagay !
तमे तो कविता करवा लाग्या !
तुम्ही तर कविता करू लागलात !
You have started composing verse.

हमारे गले यह बात नहीं उतरती.
Hamaaray galay yeh baat nahin utarti.
अमारे गळे आ वात उतरती नथी.
आम्हाला हे पटत नाही.
This thing does not appeal to us.

मेरे सोचने का तरीक़ा और है.
Mere soachne ka tareeqa aur hai.
मारी विचार करवानी रीत जुदी छे.
विचार करण्याची माझी पद्धत वेगळी आहे.
My mode of thinking is different.

अपने फ़ायदे के लिये दूसरे को नुक़सान न पहुँचाओ
Apne faaiday ke liye doosray ko nuqsaan n
  pahunchaao.
तमारा फायदा माटे बीजानुं नुकसान नहीं करो.
स्वतःच्या फायद्यासाठी दुसऱ्याचे नुकसान करू नका
Don't harm others in your interest.

हर चीज़ अपनी अहमियत रखती है.
Har cheez apni ahmiyat rakhti hai.
हरेक चीजने पोतानी अगत्य होय छे.
प्रत्येक वस्तूला स्वतःचे महत्त्व आहे.
Every thing has its own importance.

मेरे लिये यह जगह बहुत मुबारक साबित हुई.
Mere liye yeh jagah bahut mubaarak saabit hui.
मारे माटे आ स्थान घणुं लाभदायक नीवंड्युं.
मला ही जागा फायदेशीर झाली.
This place proved to be very beneficial to me.

मैं आपका मुंह मिठाई से भर दूंगा.
Men aap ka munh mithai se bhar doonga.
हुं तमारुं मों मीठुं करीश.
मी तुमचे तोंड गोड करीन.
I shall give you sweets.

अभी दिल्ली दूर है.
Abhi Dilli door hai.
हजी दिल्ली दूर छे.
अजून दिल्ली दूर आहे.
The task is still far from accomplished.

सारी रात आँखों में गुजरी.
Saari raat aankhon men guzri.
आखी रात ऊँध नही आवी.
सारी रात जागून घालविळी./सारी रात्र मला झोप नाही.
I was awake for the whole night.

उनकी आँख अभी लगी है.
Unki aankh abhi lagi hai.
तेओ हमणां ज ऊंध्या छे.
नुकताच त्यांचा डोळा लागला आहे.
He has fallen asleep just now.

आप मुझ पर क्यों बिगड़ते हैं ?
Aap mujh par kyon bigadte hain ?
तमे मारा पर शा माटे गुस्से थाओ छो ?
आपण माझ्यावर का रागावता ?
Why are you getting angry with me ?

क्या आपने मुझे अपना जर-खरीद गुलाम समझ
     रक्खा है ?
Kya aapne   mujhe apna   zar-khareed gulam
     samajh rakkha hai ?
शुं तमे मने तंमारो लखायेलो गुलाम समजो छो ?
तुम्ही मला विकत घेतलेला गुलाम समजता काय ?
Do you consider me to be your bond-slave ?

गुलामी से मौत अच्छी.
Gulaami se maut achchhi.
गुलामी करतां मोत सारुं.
गुलामीपेक्षा मरण चांगले.
Death is preferable to slavery.

जो हो सो हो.
Jo ho so ho.
थवानुं होय ते थाय.
जें व्यावयाचें असेल ते होऊ दे.
Come what may.

उसने मुझे तबाह कर दिया.
Usnay mujhe tabaah kar diya.
तेणे मने बरबाद करी नांख्यो.
त्याने मला धुळीला मिळविले.
He has ruined me.

चलो, निजात मिली.
Chalo, nijaat mili.
चालो, छटकारो थयो.
चला, सुटका झाली./सुटलो.
Well, we are free now.

उसकी सारी शेखी धूल में मिल गई.
Uski saari shaikhi dhool men mil gayee.
तेनी बधी डंफास धूळीमां मळी गई.
त्याचा सर्व अभिमान धुळीला मिळाला.
All his pride has been brought down.

चलो, क़िस्सा ख़तम हुआ.
Chalo, qissa khatm hua.
चालो, खेल खतम थई गयो.
चला, प्रकरण संपले.
Well, now the matter is over.

तुम तो उनकी हाँ में हाँ मिलाते हो.
Tum to unki haan men haan milaate ho.
तमे तो एमनी हा मां हा मिलावो छो.
तुम्ही त्याच्या होस हो देता.
You are endorsing everything he says.

तुमने उसकी मजबूरी से नाजायज़ फ़ायदा उठाया.
Tumne uski majboori se najaayaz faaida uthaaya.
तमें तेनी लाचारीनो गेरलाभ उठाव्यो.
तुम्ही त्याच्या लाचारीचा गैरफायदा घेतला.
You took undue advantage of his helplessness.

वह आपकी उदारता से नाजायज़ फ़ायदा उठाता है.
Wuh aapki udaarta se naajaayaz faida uthaata
hai.
ते तमारी उदारतानो अयोग्य लाभ उठावे छे.
तो तुमच्या उदारतेचा अयोग्य फायदा घेतो.
He takes undue advantage of your liberality.

मैं इस गुनाह बेलज्ज़त में शरीक नहीं होता.
Men is gunaah belazzat men shareek nahin hota.
हुँ आ कोरा पापनो भागीदार नहीं थाऊं
मी या निरर्थक पापात भागीदार होणार नाही.
I will not participate in this gainless sin.

यह दर्दे-सर कौन उठाये ?
Yeh darde-sar kaun uthaaye ?
आवी माथाझीक कोण करे ?
ही डोकेफोड कोणाला पाहिजे ?
Who will undertake this troublesome job ?

तुम मुझे बनाना चाहते हो ?
Tum mujhe banaana chaahate ho ?
तमे मने बनववा मागो छो ?
तुम्ही मला बनवू पाहता काय ?
Do you want to fool me ?

वह वैसे ही हवा बाँध रहा है.
Wuh vesay hi hawa baandh raha hai.
ते एम ज खोटो डौळ करे छे.
तो असना आवँ आणि असनो.
He puts up a false show.

मेरा तो यहाँ दम घुटा जा रहा है.
Mera to yahaan dam ghuta jaa raha hai.
मारो तो अहीं जीव गभराय (रुंधाय) छे
मी तर येथे गुदमरुन चाललोय.
I am feeling suffocated here.

सब रस्में अदा हो गईं.
Sab rasmen ada ho gayeen.
बधी विधिओ पूरी थईं गई.
सगळे विधि पार पडले.
All the ceremonies are over.

तुम्हारी अर्जी ज़ेर-ग़ौर है. (तुम्हारा प्रार्थना-पत्र
   विचाराधीन है)
Tumhaari arzi zair-gaur hai. (Tumhaara prarthna-
   patra vichaaraadheen hai.)
तमारी अरजी उपर विचार चाले छे.
तुमच्या अर्जीवर विचार चालू आहे.
Your application is under consideration.

आपके तो उनसे दोस्ताना ताल्लुकात हैं.
Aapkay to unse dostaana taaluqaat hain.
तमारो तो एमनी साथे दोस्तीनो संबंध छे.
आपले त्यांच्याशी मैत्रीचे संबंध आहेन.
Your relations with him are friendly.

बाज़ वक्त तुम बेतुकी बातें करने लगते हो.
Baaz waqt tum batuki baaten karne lagte ho.
कोई-कोई वार तमे ढंगधडा विनानी वातो करो छो.
कधी कधी तुम्ही विसंगत गोष्टी बोलता.
Sometimes you talk at random.

काम की शिद्दत की वजह से मेरा आना न हो सका.
Kaam ki shiddat ki wajeh se mera aana na ho saka.
कामना दबाणने लीध्रे माराथी आवी शकायुं नहीं.
काम पुष्कळ असल्यामुळे मी येऊ शकलो नाही.
I could not come due to heavy work.

आप इसमें कोई तबदीली करना चाहें तो कर सकते हैं.
Aap ismen koi tabdeeli karna chaahen to kar sakte hain.
तमे आमां कांई फेरफार करवा मागो तो करी शको छो.
आपल्याला याच्यामध्ये फरक करावयाचा असेल तर करू शकता.
If you wish to make any change in this you may.

मुझको इस पर नाज़ है. (मुझे इसका गर्व है.)
Mujh ko is par naaz hai. (Mujhe iska garva hai.)
मने आ बाबतनो गर्व छे.
मला याचा अभिमान आहे.
I am proud of it.

31. नैतिक (Moral)

ईश्वर आनन्द में है.
Ishwar anand men hai.
ईश्वर आनन्द मां छे.
ईश्वर आनन्दामध्ये आहे.
God is in joy.

साधु पुरुष का रक्षक ईश्वर है.
Sadhu purush ka rakshak ishwar hai.
साधुजननो राखणहार ईश्वर छे.
साधु पुरुषाचा रक्षक ईश्वर आहे.
God is the protector of the saintly people.

त्याग ही भोग है.
Tyaag hi bhog hai.
त्यागमां ज भोग छे.
त्याग हाच भोग आहे.
Renunciation is enjoyment.

सिर्फ़ नेक आदमी ही सुखी है.
Sirf naik aadmi hi sukhi hai.
फक्त प्रमाणिक माणस ज सुखी छे.
फक्त प्रामाणिक मनुष्यच सुखी असतो.
The virtuous alone are happy.

ज़िन्दगी सेवा के लिए है.
Zindagi sewa ke liye hai.
જિંદગી સેવાને માટે છે.
जीवन सेवेसाठी आहे.
Life is for service.

गुस्सा करना कमज़ोरी की निशानी है.
Gussaa karna kamzori ki nishaani hai.
ગુસ્સો કરવો એ નબળાઈની નિશાની છે.
रागावणे दुर्बलतेचे लक्षण आहे.
Giving way to anger is a sign of weakness.

निःस्वार्थ सेवा में बड़ा आनंद है.
Nisswaarth sewa men bada anand hai.
નિઃસ્વાર્થ સેવામાં ઘણો આનંદ છે.
निस्वार्थ सेवेत फार आनंद आहे.
There is a great joy in selfless service.

जल्दी काम शैतान का होता है.
Jaldi kaam shetaan ka hota hai.
ઉતાવળું કામ શેતાનનું હોય છે.
कामात घाई करतो तो सैतान.
Hasty work is worthy of the devil.

खाली दिमाग़ शैतान की दुकान है.
Khaali dimag shetaan ki dukaan hai.
ખાલી મન શેતાનની દુકાન છે. નવરો બેઠો નખ્ખોદ વાળે
रिकामे मन म्हणजे सैतानाचे घर.
The idle mind is the devil's workshop.

परनिन्दा दुर्गति का असाधारण कारण है.

Parninda durgati ka asaadhaaran kaaran hai.

परनिंदा दुर्गतिनुं असाधारण कारण छे.

दुर्गतीचे असाधारण कारण म्हणजे परनिंदा.

Calumny is a dreadful cause of downfall.

आलसी आदमी अध-मरे के समान है.

Aalasi aadmi adhmaray ke samaan hai.

आलसु माणस अडधो मरेला जेवो छे.

आळशी मनुष्य अर्धमेल्यासारखाच असतो.

An idle man is as good as half-dead.

हर वक्त प्रसन्न रहो.

Har waqt prasann raho.

हमेशां प्रसन्न रहो.

नेहमी प्रसन्न रहा.

Always be cheerful.

उधार न दो न लो.

Udhaar na do na lo.

उधार न लेवुं, न देवुं.

उधार देऊ नका आणि घेऊहि नका.

Neither a borrower nor a lender be.

धोखा न दो, न धोखा खाओ.

Dhoka na do, na dhoka khaao.

न छेतरो, न छेतराओ.

फसवू नका आणि फसू नका.

Neither deceive nor be deceived.

किसी से कुछ न माँगो.
Kisi se kuchh na maango.
कोईनी पासे कांई मागो नहीं.
कोणापाशी काही मागू नका.
Don't ask anything of anyone.

तुम्हें सच बात बता देनी चाहिए.
Tumhen sach baat bata deni chaahiye.
तमारे साची बात कही देवी जोईए.
तुम्ही खरी गोष्ट सांगितली पाहिजे.
You should tell the truth.

रोज़ी जिस्मानी मेहनत से कमानी चाहिए.
Rozi jismaani mehnat se kamaani chaahiye.
आजीविका शारीरिक श्रमथी मेळववी जोईए.
शारीरिक श्रमाने उपजीविका केली पाहिजे.
One should earn one's livelihood by hard work.

जो मेहनत किये बग़ैर खाता है, वह चोरी करता है.
Jo mehnat kiye bager khaata hai, wuh chori
  karta hai.
जो महेनत कर्या वगर खाय छे, ते चोरी करे छे.
जो मेहनत केल्याशिवाय खातो, तो चोरी करतो.
He who eats without earning is committing
  a theft.

जो कल के लिये जोड़ कर रखता है वह नास्तिक है.
Jo kal ke liye joad kar rakhta hai wuh naastik hai.
जे आवती कालने माटे संग्रह करे छे ते नास्तिक छे.
जो उद्यासाठी संग्रह करून ठेवतो तो नास्तिक आहे.
He who hoards for tomorrow is an atheist.

इस्लाम में सूद और शराब हराम है.
Islam men sood aur sharaab haraam hai.
इस्लाममां ब्याज अने शराब (दारू) हराम छे.
इस्लाम धर्मा मध्यें व्याज घेनें आणि दारू पिणे
निषिद्ध आहे
According to Islam it is sinful to charge interest
and to indulge in alcoholic drink.

मज़हब आपस में वैर रखना नहीं सिखाता.
Mazhab aapas men ver rakhna nahin sikhaata.
धर्म आपस आपसमां वेर करवानुं नथी शीखवतो.
धर्म आपसात वैर करायला शिकवीत नाही.
Religion does not preach enmily between man
and man.

गांधीजी का कौल था—द्वेष को प्रेम से जीतो.
Ganahiji ka qol tha—dvesh ko prem se jeeto.
गांधीजीनुं कहेवुं हतुं के द्वेषने प्रेमथी जीतो.
द्वेषाला प्रेमाने जिंका असा गांधीजी चा अुपदेश होना.
Gandhiji's motto was : "Return love for hatred."

जो कुछ करो सत्य और अहिंसा की कसौटी पर कस
कर करो.
*Jo kuchh karo satya aur ahinsa ki kasauti par
kas kar karo.*
जे कंई करो ते सत्य अने अहिंसानी कसोटी पर
कसीने करो.
जे काही कराल ते सत्य आणि अहिंसेच्या कसोटीवर
घासून करा.
Whatever you do, do it after testing it on the
touchstone of truth and non-violence.

कर्म का अटल सिद्धान्त है—जैसा करोगे वैसा भरोगे.

Karm ka atal siddhaant hai—jesa karogay vesa bharogay.

कर्मनो अटल सिद्धान्त छे के जेवुं करशो तेवुं पामशो.

जसे करावे तसे भरावे—हा कर्माचा अचूक सिद्धांत आहे.

It is an infallible doctrine of Karma : 'As you sow, so shall you reap.'

मुझे अपने फ़र्ज़ के सिवा कुछ दिखाई नहीं दे रहा.

Mujhe apne farz kay siwa kuchh dikhaayee nahin day raha.

मने मारी फरज सिवाय बीजुं कंई देखातुं नथी.

मला माझ्या कर्तव्याशिवाय काही दिसत नाही.

I don't see anything except my duty.

उसने अपने पाप का प्रायश्चित कर डाला.

Us nay apne paap ka praayashchit kar daala.

तेणे पोताना पापनुं प्रायश्चित कर्युं.

त्याने आपल्या पापाचे प्रायश्चित धेराले.

He has undergone penitence for his sin.

मैं फ़ानी चीज़ों को नहीं चाहता.

Men faani cheezon ko nahin chaahata.

मारे क्षणभंगुर चीजो नथी जोईती.

नश्वर वस्तू मला नकोत.

I don't want transitory (fugitive) things.

मेरा ज़मीर इजाज़त नहीं देता.
Mera zameer ijaazat nahin daita.
मारुं अंतःकरण मना करे छे.
माझे अंतःकरण परवानगी देत नाही.
My conscience does not permit (it).

मैं ज़िन्दगी भर ग़ाफ़िल रहा.
Men zindagi bhar gaafil raha.
हुं आखी जिन्दगी गाफेल रह्यो.
मी जीवनभर प्रमत्त राहिलो.
I remained in ignorance all my life.

प्रमाद ने मेरा नाश कर डाला.
Pramaad nay mera naash kar daala.
आळसे मारुं निकंदन काढ्युं.
आळसाने माझा नाश करून टाकला.
Indolence has ruined me.

अच्छा सत्संग रहा.
Achchha satsang raha.
सारो सत्संग रह्यो.
तथा भेटीने आनंद झाला.
It was a happy meeting.

आराम हराम है.
Aaraam haraam hai.
आराम हराम छे.
आराम हराम आहे.
To rest is to rust.
Idleness is the rust of the soul.

32. मुहावरे (Idioms)

आप तो बिलकुल ईद के चाँद हो गये हैं.
Aap to bilkul Id kay chaand ho gaye hain.
આપનાં દર્શન દુર્લભ થઈ પડ્યાં છે.
तुम्ही तर अगदी उंबराचे फूल झाला आहात.
You are rarely to be seen.

कल जलसे में खूब रंग जमा.
Kal jalsay men khoob rang jama.
કાલે જલસામાં ખૂપ રંગ જામ્યો.
काल कार्यकमाला खूप रंग चढला.
Yesterday's celebration was a glowing splen-
dour.

उनकी ग़ज़लें सुनकर दिल बाग़-बाग़ हो गया.
Unki gazalen sunkar dil baag-baag ho gaya.
તેમની ગજલો સાંભાળીને દિલ પ્રફુલ્લિત થઈ ગયું.
त्यम्र्या गझलें ऐकून मन फार प्रसन्न झाले.
His ghazals gladdened our hearts.

उसने आकर रंग में भंग डाल दिया.
Usnay aakar rang men bhang daal diya.
તેણે આવીને રંગમાં ભંગ પાડી દીધો.
त्याच्या येण्याने आनंदावर विरजण पडले.
His arrival (presence) polluted the atmosphere.

सारा मज़ा किरकिरा कर दिया.
Saaraa mazaa kirkira kar diya.
बधी मजा मारी नांखी.
सगळ्या आनंदांवर विरजण पडलें.
The whole fun has been spoilt.

मैं उड़ती चिड़िया पहचान लेता हूँ.
Men udti chidiya pehchaan leta hun.
हुं चालपरथी (माणसने) पारखी लउं छुं.
मी उडत्या पांखराची पिसे मोजणारा माणूस आहे.
I cam recognize a bird in flight.

यह हमारे बायें हाथ का खेल है.
Yeh hamaaray baayen haath ka khel hai.
आ अमारे माटे रमत जेकं छे.
हा माझ्या हातचा मळ आहे.
It is an extremely easy task for me.

आजकल उसका दिमाग़ सातवें आसमान पर है.
Aaj-kal uska dimaag saatven aasmaan par hai.
आजकल तेना अभिमाननो पारो बहु ऊंचे चढ्यो छे.
हल्ली त्याला स्वर्ग दोन बोटे उरला आहे.
He is in the seventh heaven these days.

आप ज़मीन आसमान के क़ुलाबे मिला रहे हैं.
Aap zameen aasmaan kay qulaabay mila rahe hain.
तमे आभजमीन एक करी रह्या छो.
तुम्ही आकाशपाताळ एक करता आहा.
You are linking up heaven and earth.

मुझ में आप में आकाश पाताल का अंतर है.
Mujh men aap men aakash paataal ka antar hat.
તમારામાં ને મારામાં આભજનીનનું અંતર છે.
माझ्यात आणि तुमच्यात जमीनअस्मानाचा फरक आहे.
We are poles apart.

ख्याली पुलाव पकाने से फ़ायदा ?
Khyaali pulaav pakaane se faaida ?
હવાઈ કિલ્લા ચણવાથી શો ફાયદો ?
हवेत किल्ले बांधून काय फायदा ?
What is the use of building castles in the air ?

ज़बानी जमाखर्च करने से काम नहीं चलता.
Zabaani jamaa kharch karne se kaam nahin chalta.
શેખચલ્લીનું જેવા વિચારો કરવાથી કામ નહીં ચાલે.
बोलाची कढी काय कामाची ?
Mere talk is of no avail

बीबी-बच्चे हो जाने पर सब आटे दाल का भाव मालूम
  हो जायगा.
Bibi-bachche ho jaanay par sab aate daal ka
  bhaav maaloom ho jaayega.
બાલબચ્ચાં થઈ ગયા પછી બધી ખબર પડશે.
બાલબચ્ચાં થવા દો પછી ખબર પડશે કે કેટલી
  વીશીએ સો થાય છે.
संसारात पडल्यावर सर्व काही समजून येईल.
When you have a family you will understand
  the hard realities of life.

वे अपनी डेढ़ चावल की खिचड़ी अलग ही पकाया
    करते हैं.
Way apnee dedh chaawal ki khichdi alag hi
    pakaaya karte hain.
ते पोतानो चोको जुदों राख्या करे छे.
तो अगदीं एकलकोंडा आहे.
तो एकांडा शिलेदार आहे.
He is always ploughing a lonely furrow.

आज तुम्हारा चेहरा क्यों उतर हुआ है ?
Aaj tumhaara chehra kyon utra hua hai ?
आज तमारुं मों केम पड़ी गयुं छे ?
आज तुमचा चेहरा का उतरला आहे.
Why are you sad today ?

तुम किस उधेड़बुन में पड़े हो ?
Tun kis udhedbun me pade ho ?
तमे शी भांजगडमां पडी गया छो ?
तुम्ही कोणत्या विचारात पडला आहात ?
Why are you puzzled ?

सारा मामला अभी तक खटाई में पड़ा हुआ है.
Saara maamla abhi tak khatai men pada hua hai.
आखो मामलो हजीसुधी एम ने एम अनिश्चंत पड्यो छे.
सर्व प्रकरण अद्याप भिजत पडले आहे.
The whole matter is still pending.

वह तो सुबह से ही न जाने कहाँ काफ़ूर हो गया है।

Wuh to subeh se hi na jaane kahaan kaafoor ho gaya hai.

ए तो सवारथी ज कोण जाणे क्यां रफुचक्कर थई गयो छे।

तो सकाळपासून कोठे बेपत्ता झाला आहे कोणाला ठाऊक.

He has not been seen since morning.

वह हवा का रुख देखकर चलता है।

Wuh hawa ka rukh dekhkar chalta hai.

ते जमानो जोईने वर्तें छे।

तो वारा वाहील तशी पाठ फिरवतो.

He turns his sails according to the wind.

वह तोताचश्म है।

Wuh totachashm hai.

ते कृतघ्न छे।

तो कृतघ्न आहे.

He is ungrateful.

वह इधर उधर की हाँकता रहा।

Wuh idhar udhar ki haankta raha.

ए टाढा पहोरनां गप्पा हाँकतो रह्यो।

तो थापा मारीत होता.

He kept on talking at random.

आज वह बड़ी देर तक अड्डा जमाये बैठा रहा.
Aaj wuh badi der tak adda jamaaye betha raha.
आजे ते घणो लांबो वखत अड्डो जमावीने बेसी रह्यो.
आज तो बराच वेळ धरणे धरून बसला.
Today he remained hovering over for a very
   long time.

वह मेरी जान खा गया.
Wuh meri jaan kha gaya.
ते मारो जीव खाई गयो.
त्याने माझा जीव खाल्ला.
He thoroughly exasperated me. (He bored me.)

वे हमारे हर काम में रोड़े अटकाते हैं.
*Way hamaaray har kaam men roday atkaate
   hain.*
तेओ अमारा हरेक काममां पथरा नांखे छे.
ते आमच्या प्रत्येक कामात विघ्न आणतात.
He creates hurdles in my work.

वह सबको अंगुली पर नचाता है.
Wuh sab ko anguli par nachaata hai.
ते बधाने आंगळी पर नचावे छे.
तो सर्वांना हाताच्या बोटावर नाचवितो.
He makes everybody dance to his tune.

वह मेरे पीछे हाथ धोकर पड़ा है.
Wuh mere peechhe haath dhokar pada hai.
ते मारी पाछळ खाई पीने मंड्यो छे.
तो हात धुवून माझ्या पाठीस लागला आहे.
He is doggedly after my ruination.

अब क्या नया गुल खिलने वाला है ?
Ab kya naya gul khilnewala hai ?
हवे नवुं शुं थवानुं छे ?
आता आणखी काय नवे निघणार ?
What new thing is going to happen ?

क्यों दिमाग़ चाट रहे हो ?
Kyon dimag chaat rahe ho ?
शा माटे माथुं खाव छो ?
डोके का पिकवतोस ?
Why are you pestering me ?

क्यों खामख्वाह सिर पड़ते हो ?
Kyon khaamkhwaah sir padte ho ?
शा माटे नाहक माथे पडो छो ?
उभीच माझ्या मार्थी का मारना ?
Why do you blame me without any reason ?

तुम अपने मूंह मियाँ मिट्टू बन रहे हो.
Tum apne munh miyan mitthoo ban rahe ho.
तमे जाते ज तमारां वखाण करो छो.
तुम्ही फार बढाई मारता आहात.
You are indulging in self-praise.

तुम्हारी बातें आग में घी का काम करती हैं.
Tumhaari baaten aag men ghee ka kaam karti hain.
तमारी बातो बळतामां घी उमेरे छे.
तुमचे शब्द आगीत तेल ओतण्याचे काम करतात.
Your words are adding fuel to the fire.

खाने में कितनी देर है ? यहाँ तो पेट में चहे दौड़ रहे हैं.
Khaane men kitni diar hai ? Yahaan to pait men
  choohay daud rahe hain.

जमवाने केटली वार छे ? अहीं तो पेटमां बिलाडां
  (कुरकुरियां) बोले छे.

जेवायला किती अवकाश आहे ? येथे तर पोटात
  कावळे कोकलत आहेत.

When will the food be ready ? I am feeling
  very hungry.

आज तो दावत में तुमने लड्डुओं पर खूब हाथ साफ
  किया !
Aaj to daawat men tumne ladduon pur khoob
  haath saaf kiya !

आजे जमवामां तमे लाड्डु पर ठीक हाथ चलाव्यो !

आजच्या जेवणात तुम्ही लाडवावर चांगलाच ताव
  मारला !

Today at the feast, you gave full justice to the
  'laddoos' !

तुमने इस लड़के को बड़ा सिर चढ़ा रक्खा है.
Tumne is ladke ko bada sir chadha rakkha hai.

तमे आ छोकराने बहु मोढे चढाव्यो छे.

तुम्ही या मुलाला डोक्यावर चढविले आहे.

You have given a long rope to this boy.

You have given this boy enough latitude.

उन लड़कों ने आसमान सिर पर उठा रक्खा है.
Un ladkon ne aasmaan sir pay utha rakkha hai.
ते छोकराओए तो भारे ऊधमात मचाव्यो छे.
त्या मुलांनी घर डोक्यावर घेतले आहे.
Those boys are exceedingly noisy.

इम्तहान सिर पर आ गया मगर आपको कुछ फ़िक्र नहीं.
Imtahaan sir par aa gaya magar aapko kuchh
  fikr nahin.
परीक्षा माथे अावी लागी पण तमने कांई चिन्ता नथी.
परीक्षा नोंडावर आली, तरी तुम्हाला काही काळजी
  नाही.
The examination is fast approaching, but you
  are completely indifferent to it.

उसकी असफलता ने उसकी तमाम आशाओं पर पानी
  फेर दिया.
Uski asaphalata ne uski tamaam aashaaon par
  paani phair diya.
तेनी निष्फलताए तेनी बधी आशापर पाणी फेरवी
  दीधुं.
त्याच्या अपयशाने त्याच्या सर्व आशांवर पाणी फिरले.
His failure destroyed all his hopes.

तुम्हारी बदपरहेज़ी से बीमारी ज़ोर पकड़ गई.
Tumhaari badparhaizi se beemaari zoar pakad
  gayee.
तमे परेजी नहीं पाळी एटले बीमारीए जोर पकड़्युं.
तुमच्या कुपथ्याने आजार वाढला.
Your illness worsened due to your intemperance.

अय्याशी में सब कुछ खोकर उसका दिमाग़ ठिकाने
आ गया.

*Ayyaashi men sab kuchh khokar uska dimaag
thikane aa gaya.*

विलासमां बधुं गुमावीने हवे एनी सान ठेकांणे आवी.
चेनीत सर्व काही घालविल्यावर त्याचे डोके ठिकाणा-
वर आलें.

After losing everything in luxurious living, he
has come to his senses.

बुरे लोगों का साथ देने से वे तीन तेरह नौ अठारह
हो गये.

*Buray logon ka saath dene se way teen tairah
nao athaarah ho gaye.*

खराब लोकोनी संगत करवथी तेओ बरबाद थई गया.
वाईट लोकांचा सहवास केल्यामुळे झाली त्याचे
नुकसान.

Bad company brought about their ruin.

वे तो दिनरात चैन की वंशी बजाया करते हैं.

*Way to din raat chen ki vanshi bajaaya karte
hain.*

तेओ तो रात दिवस चैननी वंशी बगाडे छे.

ते रात्रंदिवस चैन करनान.

They are leading a life of luxury.

आजकल आप निन्नानबे के फेर में पड़े हुए हैं.
Aajkal aap ninnanbe kay phair men pade huay hain.

आजकल तमे नळ्वाणुना फेरामां पड़ी गया छो.
हल्ली तुम्ही पैशाच्या मागे लागला आहा.
You are after money these days.

अमीरों के जूते चाटते रहना ही उनका धंधा है.
Ameeron key jootay chaatte rahna hi unka dhandha hai.

अमीरोनां खासडां उठाववानो ज एमनो धंधो छे.
श्रीमंतांचे पाय चाटीत राहणे हाच त्याचा धंदा आ
To flatter the rich is his only profession.

बारह बरस दिल्ली रहे क्या भाड़ झोंका ?
Baarah baras Delhi rahe kya bhaad jhonka ?

बांर बरस दिल्ली रह्या, ते शुं रळ्या ?
बारा वर्षे दिल्लीत राहून काय झक मारलीस ?
During your twelve years' stay in Delhi wh
have you achieved ?

आप आपे से बाहर क्यों होते हैं ?
Aap aapay se baahar kyon hotay hain ?

आप मनपरनो काबू केम गुमावो छो ?
तुम्ही मनावरचा ताबा का गमावता ?
Why do you lose your temper ?

आप मुझ पर क्यों आँखें लाल करते हैं ?
Aap mujh par kyon aankhen laal karte hain ?

तमे मारो सामे केम डोळा काढो छो ?
तुम्ही माझ्यावर का डोळे वटारता ?
Why do you frown at me ?

मैं तुम्हारी बन्दर-घुड़कियों से डरने वाला नहीं.

Men tumhaari bandar-ghudkiyon se darnaywala nahin.

हुं तमारी धमकी थी डरी नहीं जाऊं.

तुमच्या धमक्यांना मी भीक घालणार नाही.

I am not going to be cowed down by your threats.

मुझ पर रौब जमाने की कोशिश न करो.

Mujh par rob jamaanay ki koshish na karo.

मारा पर धाक बेसाडवानी कोशिश ना करो.

मला धाक घालण्याचा प्रयत्न करू नका.

Don't try to intimidate me.

क्यों तिल का ताड़ बनाते हो ?

Kyon til ka taad banaate ho ?

शा माटे रजनुं गज करो छो ?

राईचा पर्वत का करता ?

Why do you make a mountain out of a mo hill ?

तुम तो बात का बतंगड़ बनाते हो.

Tum to baat ka batangad banaate ho.

तमे तो वातनुं वतेसर करो छो ?

तुम्हीतर राईचा पर्वत करीत अहा.

तुम्ही पराचा कावळा करीत आहा.

You are grossly exaggerating the matter.

गड़े मुर्दे उखाड़ने से फ़ायदा ?
Gaday murday ukhaadnay se faaida ?
मरेलां मुडदां चुथवाथी शो फायदो ?
जखमेवरची खपली काढण्यात काय फायदा ?
What is the sense in ruminating the past ?

उसका दोस्त आस्तीन का साँप निकला.
Uska doast aasteen ka saanp nikla.
तेनो दोस्त दगाखोर नीकळ्यो.
त्याचा मित्र अस्तनीतला निखारा निघाला.
His friend proved treacherous.

वह नोटों का बंडल लेकर रफूचक्कर हो गया.
*Wuh noaton ka bandal laykar rafoochakkar ho
    gaya.*
ते नोटोनुं बंडल लईने रफूचक्कर थई गयो.
तो नोटांचे बंडल घेऊन पसार झाला.
He disappeared with a bundle of notes.

उसने हमारा तमाम मालमता हड़प कर लिया.
Usnay hamaara tamaam inaalmata hadap kar liya.
तेणे अमारी बधी मालमत्ता आंचकी लीधी.
त्याने आमची सारी मालमत्ता गडप केली.
He usurped all our property.

वह आँसू पीकर रह गया.
Wuh aansoo peekar rah gaya.
ते मन मारीने बेसी रह्यो.
त्याने आपले दुःख गिळले.
He swallowed the injury.

वह खून के आँसू पीकर रह जाती है.
Wuh khoon kay aansoo peekar rah jaati hai.
ते क्रोधथी समसमी रही छे.
ती असीम दुःख खोसन आहे.
She puts up with torturing grief.

वह तो अपना उल्लू सीधा करने आया था.
Wuh to apna ulloo seedha karnay aaya tha.
ए तो पोतानो स्वार्थ साधवा आव्यो हतो.
तो आपला स्वार्थ साधायला आला होता.
He had come to serve his own interest.

तुमने अपने पाँव पर आप कुल्हाड़ी मार ली.
Tumnay apnay paon par aap kulhaadi maar li.
तमे पोते ज तमारा पग पर कुहाड़ी मारी.
तुम्ही आपल्याच पायावर कुल्हाड़ीचा घाव घातलान.
You yourself have injured your cause.

डूबते को तिनके का सहारा मिल गया.
Doobtay ko tinkay ka sahaara mil gaya.
डूबताने तणखलानी सहाय मळी गई.
बुडत्याला काडीचा आधार मिळाला.
The drowning man clutched at the straw.

दोस्त वही जो वक्त पर काम आवे.
Doast wahi jo waqt par kaam aavay.
दोस्त तेज जे खरा वखते काममां आवे.
जो प्रसंगी उपयोगी पडतो, तोच मित्र खरा
A friend in need is a friend indeed

आजकल चीन की दिन दूनी रात चौगुनी तरक्की हो रही है.

Aaj kal Cheen ki din dooni raat chauguni taraqqi ho rahi hai.

आजकल चीननी दहाडे बमणी ने राते चारगणी उन्नति थई रही छे.

हल्ली चीनची झपाट्याने प्रगति होत आहे.

China is advancing by leaps and bounds these days.

भगवान जब देता है छप्पर फाड़कर देता है.

Bhagwaan jab daita hai chhappar phaad kar daita hai.

भगवान ज्यारे आपे छे, त्यारे हजार हाथे आपे छे.

अनंत हस्ते कमलावराने देता किती घेशिल दो करानी ?

When God gives he gives abundantly.

उन्होंने विरोधियों के दांत खट्टे कर दिये.

Unhonay virodhiyon kay daont khattay kar diye.

तेमणे विरोधीओना हाथ हेठा पाडी दीधा.

त्यांनी विरोधकांची खोड मोडली.

He thoroughly humbled his opponents.

जिस काम में हाथ डालो उसे पूरा करके छोड़ो.

Jis kaam men haath daalo usay poora karkay chhodo.

जे काम ने हाथमां लो तेने पूरु करीने छोडो.

ज्या कामात हात घालाल ते पूर्ण करून टाका/हाती ध्याल ते/तडीस न्या.

See that you finish whatever you undertake.

आपकी आज्ञा सिर आँखों पर.
Aap ki aagya sir aankhon par.
आपनी आज्ञा शिरोमान्य.
आपली आज्ञा शिरोधाय आहे.
I bow to your command.

तमाम किताबें हाथों हाथ बिक गईं.
Tamaam kitaaben haathon haath bik gayeen.
वधी ज चोपडीओ जोतजोतमां वेचाई गई.
सर्व पुस्तके हांतोहात विकली गेलीं.
All books were sold in no time.

लोग विज्ञान की चमत्कारिक सफलताओं पर दाँतों
    तले अँगुली दबाते हैं.
Loag Vigyaan ki chamatkaarik saphaltaon par
    daanton tale anguli dabaatay hain
लोको विज्ञाननी चमत्कारिक सफलताओ जोईने
    मोमां अंगळां नाखे छे.
लोक विज्ञानचें चमत्कृतिपूर्ण यश पाहून तोंडात बोटं
    वालतात.
People are wonder-struck at the miraculous
    achievements of science.

दुनिया बदल गई मगर आप लकीर के फकीर बने हुए हैं.
Dunia badal gayee magar aap lakeer kay faqeer
    banay huay hain.
दुनिया बधी बदलाई गई पण तमे तो एवा ने एवा
    जा रह्या.
सगळी दुनिया बदलली, पण तुम्ही होता तसेच आहां.
The world has changed but you are clinging to
    the past.

उन महलों में अब ख़ाक उड़ती है.

Un mahalon men ab khaak udti hai.

ते महेलोमां आजे धूळ उडे छे.

ते वाडे आता धूळ खात पडले आहेत.

Those palaces are now reduced to ruins.

फ़कीरी लेना टेढ़ी खीर है.

Faqeeri lena tedhi kheer hai.

फकीरी लेवी ए खांडाना खेल छे.

फकीरी म्हणजे पोरखेल नव्हे.

It is a difficult task to become a fakir.

33. कहावतें (Proverbs)

पढ़े हैं पर गुने नहीं.
Padhay hain par gunay nahin.
भण्या पण गण्या नहीं.
तो पढतमूर्ख आहे.
He is a blockhead in spite of his bookish learning.

गवाह चुस्त मुद्दई सुस्त.
Gawaah chust muddaee sust.
साक्षी पाको वादी काच्चे
साक्षी पक्का नी वादी कच्चा.
While the witness is keen, the plaintiff is indifferent.

ओछे के मुंह लगना अपनी इज्जत खोना.
Oachhay kay munh lagna apni izzat khona.
हलका साथे तकरार करी इज्जत गुमाववी.
हलकटाच्या तोंडी लागणे म्हणजे आपली अब्रू घालविणे.
To exchange words with a mean fellow is to lose one's honour.

अधजल गगरी छलकत जाय.
Adhjal gagri chhalkat jaay.
अधूरो घडो छलकाय घणो.
उथळ पाण्याला खळखळाट फार.
Empty vessel makes the most sound.

लहू लगा शहीदों में मिलना.
Lahoo laga shaheedoon men milna.
लोही लगाडीने शहीदोमां खपवुं.
रक्त लावून हुतात्मा बनणे.
To smear yourself with blood and pose as
    martyr.

नाच न जाने, आँगन टेढ़ा.
Naach na jaanay, aangan tedha.
नाचतां आवडे नहीं त्यारे आंगणुं वांकुं.
नाचता येईना, आंगण वाकडे.
A bad carpenter always blames his tools.

मान न मान मैं तेरा मेहमान.
Maan na maan men taira mehmaan.
मान न मान हुं तारो महेमान.
माना वा न माना, मी तुमचा पाहुणा.
Whether you like it or not I come as a guest.

नाम बड़े और दर्शन थोड़े.
Naam baday aur darshan thoday.
नाम मोटां ने दर्शन खोटां.
मोठे घर पोकळ वासा.
Great in reputation, petty in deed.

खोदा पहाड़ और निकली चुहिया..
Khoda pahaad aur nikli chuhiya.
खोद्यो डुंगर अने नीकळ्यो उंदर.
डोंगर पोखरून उंदीर काढला.
After all this effort you have achieved nothing.

उलटा चोर कोतवाल को डाँटे.
Ulta choar kotwal ko dante.
उपरथी चोर कोटवाळाने दंडे.
चोराच्या उलख्या बोंबा.
To turn the tables.

एक थैली के चट्टे बट्टे.
Aik theli kay chattay battay.
एक वेलनां तुंबडां.
एकाच माळेचे मणी.
Birds of the same feather.

नौ सौ चूहे खाय बिल्ली हज को चली.
Nau sau choohay khai billi haj ko chali.
सो उंदीर मारीने बिल्ली हज करवा चाली.
करून सवरून भागले आणि पूजेला लागसे.
It is easy to preach fasting on a full belly. To sermonise on fasting after feasting.

चार दिन की चाँदनी फिर अंधेरी रात.
Chaar din ki chaandni phir andheri raat.
चार दिननी चांदनी पछी अंधारी रात.
नव्याचे नऊ दिवस.
A nine days' wonder.

हाथ कंगन को आरसी क्या ?
Haath kangan ko aarsi kya ?
हाथे कंकण ने आरसीनी शी जरूर ?
हातच्या कंकणाला आरसा कशाला ?
A self-evident truth needs no proof.

हंडिया का एक चावल देखा जाता है.
Handia ka aik chaaval daikha jaata hai.
खीचड़ोनो एक ज दाणो चांपी जोवाय.
शितावरून भाताची परीक्षा करता येते.
To judge a crop from a single ear.

काठ की हाँडी बार-बार नहीं चढ़ती.
Kaath ki haandi baar-baar nahin chadhti.
लाकडानी हांल्ली वारे वारे ना चढे.
लाकडाची हंडी पुन्हा चुलीवर ठेवतां येत नाहीं.
Wouldst thou have a serpent, sting thee twice ?

दमड़ी की हाँडी गई, कुत्ते की जात तो पहचानी.
*Damdee ki haandi gayee, kuttay ki zaat to
pahechaani.*
दमडीनी हांल्ली गइ, पण कुतरानी जात तो ओळखी.
दमडीचे मडके गेले, पण कुत्र्याची जात तर कळली.
We get the measure of a man from the way he
bears a trifling loss.

गुड़ खाय गुलगुलों से परहेज.
Gud khaay gulgulon se parhaiz.
कढी खाय पण कढीमांनी वडीनी परेजी.
गुळ खातो नी गुलगुव्याचे पथ्य करतो.
To swallow a camel, and strain at a gnat.

मुंह में राम बगल में छुरी.
Munh men ram bagal men chhuri.
मुखमां राम बगलमां छुरी.
तोंडी रामनाम आणि काखेत सुरी.
A honeyed tongue but a heart of gall.

नक्कारखाने में तूती की आवाज़.

Naqqaarkhanay men tooti ki aawaaz.

नगारामां पिपूडीनो अवाज.

नगाऱ्यापुढे टिमकी.

What avails the warbling of a nightingale in the
    midst of an uproarious din !

हाथी के दाँत खाने के और दिखाने के और.

Haathi kay daant khaanay kay aur dikhaanay
    kay aur.

हाथीना दांत चाववाना जुदा अने देखाडवाना जुदा.

हत्तीचे दात दाखवायचे निराळे आणि खायचे निराळे.

A hypocrite pretends to be what he is not.

पानी मथने से घी नहीं निकलता.

Paani mathne se ghee nahin nikalta.

पाणी वलोव्याथी घी नहीं नीकळे.

पाणी घुसळले म्हणून लोणी निघत नाही.

Puddles yield no pearls, however deep you may
    dive in.

ज्यों ज्यों दवा की, मर्ज़ बढ़ता गया.

Jyon jyon dawa ki, marz badhta gaya.

जेम जेम दवा करता गया, रोग वधतो गयो.

औषधोपचाराबरोबर रोग वाढत गेला.

The disease grew worse, the more it was treated.

मन के लड्डुओं से भूख नहीं मिटती.

Man kay laddoouon se bhookh nahin mitti.

मनना मोदकथी भूख नहीं भागे.

मनातले मांडे खाऊन भूक भागन नाहीं.

It is no use building castles in the air.

ओस चाटे प्यास नहीं बुझती.
Oas chaatay pyaas nahin bujhti.
हाथ चाटे पेट नहीं भराय.
दात कोरून पोट भरत नाही.
Dew-drops can't quench one's thirst.

दिन ईद रात शबे-बरात.
Din Id raat Shabe-Baraat.
दिन-रात दिवाली.
सदासर्वंकाळ दिवाळी.
Every day is a feasting day.

जो गरजते हैं सो बरसते नहीं.
Jo garajtay hain so barastay nahin.
गाज्या मेह वरसे नहीं.
गजेल तो पडेल काय.
Barking dogs seldom bite.

अपनी अपनी ढपली अपना अपना राग.
Apni apni dhapli apna-apna raag.
पोतपोताना तानमां मस्त.
आपली टिमकी अन् आपलाच राग.
Many heads, many minds.

एक और एक ग्यारह होते हैं.
Aik aur aik gyaarah hoatay hain..
बे मळे बावन वीर, एकनां करतां बे भला.
संघशक्तीने कार्य साधते.
Union is strength.

गया वक़्त फिर हाथ आता नहीं.
Gaya waqt phir haath aata nahin.
गयो वखत फरी पाछो आवतो नथी.
गेला काळ परत येत नाहीं.
Time and tide wait for no man.

एक तन्दुरुस्ती हज़ार नियामत.
Aik tandurusti hazaar niyaamat.
पहेलुं सुख तो जाते नयां.
आरोग्य होच खरी संपत्ति.
Health is wealth.

जुबाँ शीरीं मुल्कगीरी.
Zubaan sheereen mulkgeeree.
जेनी जीभ पर अमी तेने दुनिया समी.
बोले गोड त्याला सगळे धड.
A sweet tongue conquers the world.

आप भला तो जग भला.
Aap bhala to jag bhala.
आप भला तो जग भला.
आपण भंले तर जग भले.
To the good the world appears good.

जैसी नीयत वैसी बरकत.
Jesi neeyat vesi barkat.
जेवी दानत तेवी बरकत.
जशी दानत तशी बरकत.
Like mind, like find.

जैसा करना वैसा भरना.
Jesa karna vesa bharna.
जेवु करे तेवुं भरे.
कारवे तसे भरावे.
You shall reap as you sow.

सुने सबकी करे मन की.
Sunay sab ki kare man ki.
सांभळो सौनुं, करो मननुं.
ऐकावे जनाचे, करावे मनाचे.
Lend your ear to all but follow your own
    counsel.

सोने में सुगंध.
Sonay men sugandh.
सोनामां सुगंध.
दुधात साखर.
It's a paradise on earth.